the lost Love

. . . .

Michael Lanfield

We Are Interconnected, 2016

To all the nonhuman animals for whom this book is written.

Acknowledgments

· · · · · · · · · · · · · · · · · ·

This book wouldn't have been made possible without the support of my friends, family and followers and to Jahara Rhiannon for proofreading. I wish to thank my very good friends Paul, Felicia, and Lena, for all the years of friendship, support and love. If it weren't for my friend Laura and her love and perseverance for the fight on behalf of animals, I wouldn't be writing this today. I am very thankful for her love, friendship, and support. She was the first person I ever worked with as an activist. She was very kind, welcoming me with open arms. I also want to thank Pig Save, for giving me the opportunity bearing witness on many accounts, awakening me to a new level of understanding and consciousness. A big thank you to all activists everywhere, for creating a kinder and more just world for everyone.

I cannot forget to acknowledge my uncle Jan, my mom and aunt Niki for all the support and love as well. And I am also very grateful to the universe for giving me this gift of life and opportunity to express the truth and knowledge to the world.

And lastly, to everyone who picked up this book and is now reading it, much obliged to you. All I ask is that you read it with an open-mind and take in all the information, even if it not to your liking.

Table of Contents

Introduction

. . . .

What you are about to read is eye-opening, yet, it is the harsh reality and truth that few people want to face. Because of our cultural indoctrination, The Lost Love has been hidden and suppressed within us since infancy, literally for thousands of years, and now is awaiting for us to reawaken to the truth that we are: eternal spiritual beings.

This book contains many controversial issues and truths that many people might not want to embrace. However, if we do not adopt these ideas, we may be faced with a tragic aftermath or even a demise of all life on the planet. Though many people already understand these ideas, the majority of us have not embraced them.

The book you are about to read is the sequel to my first; *The Interconnectedness of Life*. I refer to a lot of passages and ideas from that book, and so I highly recommend reading it also.

The Lost Love sets us on a journey, a spiritual path to awareness and awakening. As our journey progresses, one may find themselves becoming a healthier and happier person. It may even lead to new and exciting opportunities. This book is not about health, nutrition or new age spirituality, but rather words of wisdom that will reawaken love into our lives and view the world in a whole new perspective.

The missing piece, of *The Lost Love*, can bring about significant changes that raise the collective consciousness on our planet. There is no better time than now to embrace the ideas that will bring about global peace and harmony to humankind. It is such a tragedy that most spiritual teachers and authorities preach these ideas, yet fail to manifest them into their lives. These ideas are ancient teachings that stem back all the way to the very beginnings of human civilization. However, because of our human conditioning over the last 10,000 years, it has been lost, or rather suppressed, within us.

Wise spiritual masters are usually the ones who awaken to the message. Those who have not embraced these ideas, often die sick, miserable deaths. These concepts are not new to most people. They have been adopted by wise men such as Leonardo DaVinci, Pythagoras, Albert Schweitzer, Leo Tolstoy, and Plato.

I have compiled all of the truths in one short, easy to read book. I understand because of the delicate subject matter, some readers may dismiss a few of the ideas as pure naïveté or untruths. This might be the case because most people are bombarded and programmed in the current system of violence, and they cannot distinguish real truth from falsehood. Even if one disagrees with some of the ideas presented, that is not a reason to dismiss the book in its entirety. It is an honor to present *The Lost Love* and the ideas that make up this book. Lie back and relax, and let the journey begin.

1
Interconnectedness

. . . .

We are all interconnected. In his book *The Divine Matrix*, Gregg Braden goes into the science of how this is so.[1] That energy here relates to energy elsewhere in the world. A person, for example, can affect another person, or a tree or a nonhuman animal on the other side of the world. People have healed others just by thought and feeling alone. No medical interventions came into play at all. And this happens even when the healer is not in the same room with the patient.[2]

Though energy changes, the energy here is the same as energy elsewhere on the planet. It is all interconnected. The force is in me, it is in front of me, it is out there everywhere, and also in every other being. Energy is everywhere. There is no place that energy does not exist. Even in inanimate objects, there is energy.

Energy, energy-field, energy-body, life force, or universe, because the universe is made up of energy and energy, therefore, is the universe. Let me explain. Every living being came from one energy source. Whether it was the big bang or god, we all came from one energy source, and that source eventually turned into light. At first, this universal energy source may have been created out of darkness, but eventually, it turned into light. It was a source that created the most primitive life-forms, the smallest microbes. Eventually, other more advanced life-forms started appearing, until the primitive nonhuman animal manifested. Later, more advanced types of animal life forms emerged, and it evolved and was created into what we know today as Homo sapiens, modern human-animal.

So even though other species may look and seem different, in the external reality we are all the same; we are all interconnected. Energy is everywhere. It is external, and it is also internal within ourselves. So, because of the universe, the energy-field that is all around and inside ourselves, we possess all the knowledge and truths of the universe. However, we may not understand what the truths and knowledge are, because, to know the truth and teachings that lie buried deep within our hearts, we need to awaken to the truth that we are, that of love. That is why many of us are searching for answers and cannot find them. Because we must first become love. And for many people, likely the majority of us, we have not cultivated love yet. It lies dormant within our souls. We have yet to awaken.

And even though we possess all the knowledge and truth within our hearts', we act contrary to our hearts yearning for love. Our thoughts and our actions are that of violence, even though we may not believe so.

The universe contains all the knowledge and truths there are. And we cannot awaken to all truths and understanding, even though we possess all the knowledge and truths within. I believe there are no super beings alive on this or any other planet or galaxy. This is because of our ever expanding Buddha-nature. We are ever learning more new truths and raising our consciousness, and no one can understand or know everything. This universal energy-field is ever expanding, it is vast and infinite. We can learn, and we can acknowledge, and become more aware and raise our consciousness to a higher level and awaken to the truths that lie within our hearts and the vast universe. The more awakened and aware we are of the truth that we are, adds another piece to the puzzle, the mystery of life itself.

And so, all of this comes down to love. Love is the key. It is the key to uncovering the truths that lie within our hearts, to uncovering the knowledge, the wisdom, and the compassion. We are love. We contain everything, all the energy, and we are in everything. It is so because we are all interconnected as we came from the same source. Even though at the time we were all part of the same source, as one unit, today we believe we are separate, according to our perception of the external reality. However, we did not separate because the universal energy-field can never be separated. It is everywhere and in everyone and everything. Energy once again is everywhere, and it cannot be destroyed because of the law of conservation of energy.[3]

We see everything as a separate unit, because in the present external reality when we see a tree, a dog or another human being, we believe they are separate only due to our perception of the external. In my view, this is not true reality as it may be only our perception of what we believe to be true reality. Just as we perceived at one point in history, that the earth was flat, or that the earth was at the centre of the universe. Today we know that is not true. Our perceptions change over time. So whatever we perceive to be true in the current external reality, might not be so. It may just be a perception of our belief of what we think the reality is at that moment. This is why when we sense a deep revelation from within and awaken to the truth and wisdom, we feel love.

How do we know what truth is, though? Truth cannot be obtained from books or religions, through family traditions or any institutions. Though I agree that some teachings and truths are obtainable through books or with the help of others, ultimately, the truth is felt within the heart once we start becoming aware and awakened to what love is. Once we find true love within our hearts and send that love out to all beings, in thought and practice, then will we be blessed with the truth.

Positive Emotions

able, abundant, awake, aware, beautiful, calm, peaceful, compassion, love, empathy, conscious, joyful, happy, free, kind, harmony, helpful, honest, selflessness, sharing, trusting, equal, wise lost, cheat, jealous, abuse, afraid, skeptical, untrusted, scared, defensive, inferior, worthless, negativity, insecure, violence, fear, trap, lie, unsupported, judge, hurt, suffer, kill, hate

As you can see from the above charts, there are words that either causes positive or negative emotions. I could have listed many more, but just to give you an idea, the word love, for example, is a positive emotion and vibration and when it is felt deep in the heart we feel joy and happiness. However, when we exert violence over another being, directly or indirectly, we feel a negative emotion, and it makes us feel terrible deep in our hearts. Though the negative feeling is still felt within our bodies and heart, we might not necessarily feel the emotion immediately on the outer level. Even if we do feel the aftermath of it, we usually attribute the cause of our suffering with external worldly affairs, genes, old age or something else. Let's look at one situation for example. When a person unconsciously harms another being by purchasing the flesh and secretions of tortured animals, the result of such vile action may not be felt for many weeks, months or even years after the action took place. And it is also unlikely and very rare that people connect their suffering to the torture and death of innocent beings they cause harm to. Therefore, misery, depression, illness, disease, and very frequently even death occurs at some later point in the person's life. This is what is known as "as you sow, so shall you reap", "karma", "the boomerang effect", or "cause and effect." Therefore, it is wise that we stick at all times to positive emotions, thoughts, and actions that of unconditional love for all beings. And again, love is the key. Love solves all problems.

> "When we consume animals for whom this consumption means fear, mutilation, imprisonment, and death, we also inflict great pain upon ourselves, as these vibrations of fear affect us."[4]
> **Kim Deborah Benson (Presh)**

Over the eons of time, man has been at war. He has perpetuated violence throughout history, and we see today we are still at war with one another. There is violence everywhere we turn; in movies and video games, on television and in the media and news, in magazines and books, and the internet. And it doesn't stop there. Most of all, because of our food choices and forced cultural indoctrinations, of the herding culture, trillions of innocent beings die annually.[5] Consequently, we are faced with the biggest aftermath of all. Because of the excessive breeding, use, and killing of animals, it is causing tremendous suffering and violence on a whole range of fronts in the world today. There is currently a major health epidemic around the world where people are succumbing to heart disease, cancer, diabetes, the flu, and other major diseases and illnesses. We live in a world where tens of thousands of children starve every single day and human trafficking and slavery still happen on the greatest scale ever.[6] Animal agriculture uses the most water and oil compared to any other industry, and it is also the key player in environmental devastations such as climate change, soil erosion, desertification, and deforestation.[7] And the list does not stop there. In my previous book, I describe how evil animal agriculture is on a grand scale. We also cannot forget that racism, sexism, homophobia, transphobia, ableism, and other forms of discrimination still exist. Will we ever solve any of the world issues, by continuing to be part of the herding culture, using, and killing animals?

Love is a positive emotion. And, as a result, we feel happy. When we love, first ourselves and then all others, it brings us joy. That is what people are missing; happiness. Religion teaches us that when we die our spirits go to heaven, and only then will we experience happiness.[8] Why can't we feel happy now? Why do we have to wait for god or for the ascent to heaven to find happiness? Don't we understand that we possess love within us? When we exhibit love for all sentient beings, that is when we will find true happiness. And only then, will we be happy.

When we feel hate, fear or exert violence on another, which are all negative and dark emotions, our entire body contracts, including our heart and mind. As human beings we turn towards light; any lit object such as the sun, the brightly lit moon, sunrises and sunsets, and even towards the artificial light. This is because our innate spiritual being is that of love. We cannot deny this. Love and happiness are light, and hate, fear, violence, suffering, and death are all darkness.

No one feels true happiness from negative emotions or causing the suffering or death to another, even if it is only in thought. Thoughts manifest into external reality, and even though a thought is just a thought, all thoughts are formed in both the mind and the heart which contains energy.

Some people claim that there is no such thing as good or evil, positive or negative. Therefore, everything is neutral, or at least, we should possess neutral thoughts. This is a very wrong position to take. This is not the truth. Let's take a look at one scenario for example. Let's say we are walking down the street, and a group of criminals is stealing money from an elderly person, or maybe someone is hitting a helpless child on the street, or maybe it is their dog they are abusing. Instinctively, we would try to help the poor victim, because we know in our hearts the act of violence is wrong, because as mentioned before, as human-animal beings we turn to light, not darkness. We turn to love, not violence. When we help another being in need, we help turn darkness into light. We don't condemn the one who is causing harm to the victim, but rather love them. Why? Because we are light beings and any negative (dark) emotions, thoughts or feelings towards anyone, brings about more hate, violence, and darkness into this world.

We understand that there is much suffering in this world. Spiritual masters understand that to heal darkness and suffering; we must not fight it, but rather bring more light into it. Thus, we need to create a new world based on love, kindness, and compassion. Many spiritual masters also understand that the meaning of life is "Unconditional love" and "Non-violence".

> "I object to violence because when it appears to do good, the good is only temporary; the evil it does is permanent."
> **Mahatma Gandhi,** Indian political leader

When young children play with one another, they exhibit pure joy and happiness. And they smile, and they laugh. It is love that they feel. It is only once we've been conditioned by our parents, family, and friends, educational systems, and various institutions, that we find ourselves drifting away from joy, happiness, and love. Instead, we are taught to compete and be indifferent to one another, and be speciesist towards nonhuman animals. Though we may love our cats and dogs, we stick forks and knives into other animals who are just as deserving of our love.

We attend school when we are young; the education system teaches us what they want us to learn. They never teach us about the universe, spirituality or truths and knowledge. The public-school educational system is also a part of the problem. Yes of course we are taught useful and important skills such as reading, writing, and arithmetic. However, ultimately, these are of no use to our essential nature; whose drive is to seek truth and wisdom from within. It is only a good thing temporarily, as we are still part of the dominant culture of exploitation, suffering, and death.

Of course, in an imperfect world such as ours, none of us are perfect. Whilst we might strive to be perfect, trying to not cause harm, sometimes it is unavoidable. The key is to cause the least harm whenever possible. This is where love comes in. If we unconditionally love all beings, through our thoughts and actions, eventually even the unavoidable actions will become avoidable. But we shouldn't worry too much about this, because once we start loving, the universe takes care of the unintentional harm.

What we see in the external, the world around us, is the product of what is going on in the internal, within ourselves. So, if we see a lot of violence around us, it is because we still need to heal a part of ourselves. This hurt we experience on a deep subconscious level might even be the karmic retribution that we may have had from previous lives. Again, energy out all around us is the same as the energy within us. Yes, energy changes, but energy is the same out there, as it is inside of us.

People believe that they are not causing any suffering. They think they are honest, good people. Yes, on the outside they may seem like honest and caring people. But when we analyze their lives, are they honest, good people, when they pay farmers and slaughterhouse workers to torture and kill animals? Though deep in our hearts, we all possess love, some people haven't awakened to the love. And so, they unconsciously, pay and support the use and killing of animals.

Many vegans are outraged at such people. To my disbelief, I see many mean and utterly vile comments about wanting to jail such people and even comments such as "I want their balls cut off", or "kill all these abusers." These comments are coming from people who should be loving and caring towards all beings. What these vegans seem to forget, is that most of them were once animal abusers as well. Most, if almost all vegans, grew up eating animal foods. It was nothing they ever did on their own. As infants, we were programmed to consume animal foods; the flesh, dairy, eggs, and honey from extremely abused animals. From the baby food jars in supermarkets, containing chicken, lamb and cheese, to our brothers and sisters feeding us small pieces of animal flesh.

As innocent young children, our parents and family force us to consume certain foods even if it goes against our natural instinct. Deep down, some kids know what they are eating, and protest to try not to eat. We are not informed as to where the food comes from, as a lot of adults do not know. Intuitively, though, as youngsters, we understand that we would rather pet and hug animals than kill them for food.

This is the same as doctors circumcising newborn babies. Against their will, babies are taken away and forced, without consent, and with their parent's permission, to be circumcised. This is an extremely painful procedure where the end of the foreskin is cut off without any anesthesia. They are also given all sorts of vaccinations against their will. In animal agriculture, they do a similar producer to pigs and other animals called castration. This by far is the most horrific procedure done to newborns. It is shown that infants feel pain even more acutely than adults. And these procedures, done on both pigs and human children, are totally unnecessary.

People ask me, "If nothing exists, why even bother?" or "The world will eventually end anyways!" These are very negative attitudes to take. And that is why many people are not happy. We all understand because we are love if anyone suffers we must help them. We also know, because we care about the environment, we must not throw garbage or plastic just anywhere, but dispose of them properly. We know that if there is some injustice we have to be the guardian because caring for others is what creates true happiness.

In 2009, when I had the spiritual awakening (which you can read more about in my book *The Interconnectedness of Life*), I felt scared at first because I didn't know what was happening. As my psyche started awakening, I felt connected to the birds, to the trees, insects, clouds, the sun, stars, and all the rest of creation. I finally understood, because we are all interconnected and that I was in all other living beings, they were also in me. And if I caused harm to another being I would also be causing harm to myself.

One cannot explain a revelation. And so one has to experience it for themselves. If we don't unconditionally love all beings, I mean even love for fishes, flies, and snakes, we haven't awakened at all. We may certainly be aware that we need to preserve our environment and be kind to one another. Some people may even consider these to be awakenings. However, if our hearts are not that of unconditional love for all of creation, we haven't even started awakening.

Religion, especially Christianity, teaches followers that god created all life on this planet. And because god created animals, both human and nonhuman and the environment, that god is in every creature and all living things. If we do not love god's creatures, we do not love god. God is within all beings and therefore, when we are indifferent and harmful to god's creation, we harm a part of god. This is why most believers are sinners.

Before atheists jump up in protest, I would like to explain the notion of god and the universe. Human beings created the concept of god. An imaginary figure that resembles an older Caucasian man high up in the sky with a greyish/white beard who created all life on this planet. However, this is an egotistical way of portraying god that positions humans as superior to all other beings on Earth: Humans deferring only to the alleged authority of this 'god' and to religious texts such as the Bible, which allegedly represents truth. But truth can only come from within, when we have cultivated love. In my view, the true god is the universe. One and the same. God is also made up of energy just like the rest of us. And therefore, we all possess god within us, which I like to call our Buddha-nature. That is why at times I use the word 'god' and 'universe' interchangeably, and why I do not capitalize the word god. 'God' is neither human or animal, but rather an energy form of our higher consciousness. And the universe is all "existing matter and space considered as a whole; the cosmos."

And because god and the universe are both one and the same, we don't have to be scared of god or even using the word. To most people, god is a supreme, all-just, all-caring Being, who is greater than human-kind. But in reality, that Being is us. Don't forget that we possess the universe or god within ourselves. We hold all the knowledge and truth. As a result, people, especially atheists are outraged when I mention or discuss the god concept, universe, spirituality, etc. Because most atheists do not believe in any of this, or at least in the notion of god.

As for religion, I have nothing against it. I am only in nonsupport of institutions, like religion, which are part of the herding culture, which supports and validates the consumption of animals with church barbeques and dinners. I think they hideously reinforce the idea that we can continue worshiping god or Jesus while continuing to use, exploit, and kill other innocent beings.

This book is about truth, not belief systems that do not reside within the Anahata or heart chakra. This book does not concern itself with the debate between religious fundamentalists and atheists over whether god exists. This book's basis and ideas come from within the heart, which is pure unconditional love. This is the truth. Everything else is false programming if the basis of the teaching is part of the herding mentality.

> Herding animals – sounds similar to "hurting animals."

The statistics are shocking, it seems that 97 to 99.99 percent of all animals on the planet are killed for food. Despite this, nothing is being done about it.

Ultimately, it comes down to *whom* we eat. Humans consume the flesh and secretions of brutally tortured and murdered beings who have never done anything to us. When anyone manages to get close enough to wild animals, for the animals to see and smell the human, their natural instinct is to run. More often than not, these animals are unable to escape the bullets and traps.

People often say it is corporations and governments who are at fault. It is not really about other beings. It is the GMOs and the pesticides and all the tainted foods in supermarkets. And they blame Monsanto and the large multinationals as the problem. But humans created the problems, not corporations. We started out herding animals 10,000 years ago. We are the ones that started viewing them, especially female animals and their reproductive organs, as property and slaves. Thousands of years later, we started owning human beings as slaves and women were treated unfairly like property. And yes, though I agree, corporations are at fault for false advertising and misleading the general public, ultimately it is humans who are to blame. Thousands of years ago there were no corporations, but still we were waging wars on each other.

The animals that we raise for food, no matter how well they are treated, even if raised organically or humanely, free-range, grass-fed, Halal, Kosher or even in our backyard, are still considered property. These are just labels used within the industry. Even in the nicest conditions, and letting them live their full lives, we steal their eggs, milk, and honey and eventually take their lives. As we do this year after year, it ends up killing us.

When one being is killed, it harms the whole. We destroy the rainforests to graze livestock and grow food to feed to the animals. In turn, we harm starving humans, by feeding the grains and legumes to the animals that could otherwise feed people directly. Afterwards, innocent beings are trucked off to the slaughterhouse, where people then have to slaughter hundreds or even thousands of animals on a daily basis. And this is not good for them, as slaughterhouse workers many of them turn to alcohol and drugs, and it leads to spousal and child abuse. And then they go out and do the same horrible things in their communities.[9, 10]

We then eat the animals, which causes vibrations of suffering and death throughout our bodies, on all levels

– spiritual, mental, and physical. Later, animal cholesterol, fat, and acidifying protein in meat, dairy, and eggs cause cancers, diabetes, strokes, heart disease, and other illnesses. While we try figuring out where we went wrong, we put a band-aid on the situation by giving ourselves pills and perform procedures that treat symptoms rather than causes. Lastly, we again blame governments and corporations, GMOs, pesticides, and pollution, so we take heaps of supplements thinking that this must be the solution. If everyone on the planet ate a standard Western diet high in animal products, we would need at least two, maybe even as many as fifteen planets just to sustain our addiction.

In the end, if nothing truly exists in the external world, why then bother helping anyone? It comes back to love and happiness. Even if nothing were to exist in the world around us, it matters to the individual who is suffering. If you were suffering, wouldn't you want someone to help you, heal you, hug you, and love you? When we assist the needy, the sick, and the dying, it creates happiness. Happiness is what humans lack. And this is our ultimate purpose; to love and be happy.

But can one person really make a difference in this world? It comes down once more to the interconnectedness of all life. As we contain all the energy, knowledge and truths within us, we also contain all living things as well. And because we contain all energy-matter, as we awaken to love and start actively teaching others the truths, we send ripples out into the cosmic vastness, raising global consciousness. This is what is needed; to raise global consciousness on a massive scale.

Therefore, one person does make a difference. Let me explain it in another way. Each of us is like a grain of sand or a drop of water in the ocean. If that one drop of water or grain of sand does not exist and another one does not exist and another and so on, then there will be no sandy beach or ocean. And if the ocean or beach does not exist, life will not exist. However, on the contrary, if we do awaken to love, but do not teach others these truths, then we cannot start to raise global consciousness. Even though it is possible to meditate and pray and do all the inner work, we must also do the outer work as well, spreading the message of love and compassion. It is sad to see many vegan Buddhist monks doing the inner work, but they never seem to do the outer work. How do we expect to raise global consciousness through inner work alone?

As I previously stated, when you send out love to the universe, let the universe take care of the rest. Again, this is only when we cause unavoidable harm. In most situations, when we avoid harm we still need to do the outer work, educating those who are unaware and unawakened. It is just like soil. If a seed is not planted, a flower does not grow. Thus, the soil in this example represents humanity; the seed represents love in a human, and the flower signifies the awakening. When we plant a seed of love within an individual, that seed will grow into a plant (awakening), or that seed (love) will not sprout. Our job is not to get the seed to germinate; we need to plant the seed with tender loving care and let that seed do its job. It may be that some people awaken only after hundreds or thousands of seeds have been planted within them. When it comes to family and friends, it is harder to plant seeds of love. It is therefore recommended by many activists, to educate the general public and people who are more open-minded.

"When the suffering of another creature causes you to feel pain, do not submit to the initial desire to flee from the suffering one, but on the contrary, come closer, as close as you can to him who suffers, and try to help him."[11]
Leo Tolstoy, Russian writer

2
Do Plants Feel Pain?

. . . .

Before anyone shouts, "But don't plants feel pain too?" In my view, both plants and animals are able to experience discomfort. But the suffering of plants and animals are not the same. If we compare plant foods to a standard animal-based diet, the latter causes a far greater destruction of life. Every diet causes harm, but a vegan diet (better yet, a fruitarian diet), causes the least harm. It is still not an excuse to not embrace veganism, though. Not only does an animal-based diet kill trillions of innocent beings as aforementioned, up to sixteen pounds of grains are consumed for every one pound of flesh produced.[1] So we consume more plants on an animal-based diet. Vegans rather, eat a smaller portion of plants compared to this number. Even if we were to take into account, the

> "It is true that all plants are conscious to an extent, but they are far less conscious than an animal."[2]
> **Kim Deborah Benson (Presh)**

transportation of the plant foods from overseas, it still would not equate to the amount of fossil fuels, water, land, and other intense resources required for animal agriculture.

Even though it is proven by science that plants do not contain a central nervous system, we understand, that all living things can suffer to some degree.[3] However, just because plants may have the ability to suffer, does not mean we should disregard the suffering of animals. As intelligent human beings when we step on a dog's tail, he or she whimpers in pain. We know when we stub our toe that we feel pain, or when we put a knife into a cow, or chicken, that that being is experiencing excruciating pain. We cannot argue this.

Most people understand the difference when it comes to the suffering of animals and the use of plants for food. However, we act contrary to this and still justify the consumption of animal foods based

> "There's a thing about growing plants (that was typically women's work) and brings out the best in us in a sense of working with nature and with the cycles of life and with the abundance and creativity of life."[4]
> **Will Tuttle, PhD,** Author of *The World Peace Diet*

on the plants feel pain argument. This is hypocritical.

Humans and nonhuman animals are mobile with the ability to move about. Plants do not. They are not able to flee from predators and do not have an evolutionary need to be mobile. And because of this, animals have the evolutionary need to experience the sort of discomfort and pain, which plants are not capable of. As we humans start loving all beings, we know that taking the life of an animal is very different from picking fruit or tending to a garden. One is an act of violence while the other is living in harmony with all life. Gently plucking fruit from a tree, eating it mindfully, and dispersing of the seeds in nature, is a symbiotic natural life-affirming process, unlike the killing of nonhuman animals, which is an act of violence.

3
Owning Animals

· · · · · · · · · · · · · · · · · · ·

When it comes to other animals, we first need to understand the consequences of using them in the first place. Many people lack the ability to think critically. In fact, most, if not all humans are not highly spiritually evolved or conscious. They live their lives not aware of wars raging around the world or slaughterhouses where millions of animals are tortured and killed. Even though people are half asleep, they believe everything they experience is a natural state of being. They believe they are awakened, they know the truths and that they are free thinkers with the ability to do as they please.

It is because we are conditioned from such a young age, by our culture, eating the same way, year after year, and decade after decade, that we never question our habits. We continue justifying the violence like it causes no harm to anyone. Why? Why do we cause so much suffering in the first place and where did it come from?

In my quest to uncover the truth, I set out to seek the answer. Of course, all the knowledge lies within our being. And even if we have awakened to truth and love, sometimes, we need to look elsewhere for further insight. Again, through books or teachings from others, it can certainly guide us to love. Ultimately, love arises from the heart.

Many ages ago, at the time of the herding culture, some of us humans, felt as if we lacked something in our lives. We were bored and wanted change. When we started herding large animals together, especially female animals, for our benefit, it was a system of domination and violence against other beings. During this time, we started causing suffering to others. Yes, we ate the flesh of animals for hundreds of thousands of years, but only for necessity and survival. We did not cause deliberate suffering to those beings.

The violence began mainly due to the need for survival. We were gatherers for most of our evolutionary history. We gathered all types of fruits; even on occasion some nuts, seeds, and leafy greens. When fruits were scarce, root vegetables and maybe even tubers and sea vegetables were available.

Only when we started migrating north, and the availability of plants began to diminish did we consume the flesh of animals. Why we ever migrated north from the tropics in the first place is a widely debated topic. I believe when we started eating the flesh of animals, we did not hunt them but rather ate whatever food we could find to sustain ourselves. We were scavengers at the time, and apart from some plant foods, had only the flesh of the dying, old, and young animals. As we migrated further north to colder climates, we were in search of food and ways to keep ourselves warm. We used animals for food and clothing for basic survival.

Following this (starting around 384 BCE), we also

started using nonhuman animals for vivisection, entertainment, and so on.[1] And later, humans were used as entertainment, as slaves and servants to others. At this time, women also became the property of men. We have come to accept violence, and even consider ourselves to be a violent species. Violence is very much a part of our culture, so much that we have fallen in love with it. There is so much suffering and violence all around us that we believe Eden to be inconceivable. We will never get there so let's not even try at all. We will only get to an Edenly Heaven once we pass on.

As our hearts and minds shift from violence to love, there can be no "use" of animals that is acceptable. The idea of using another being for our advantage goes against our moral values. There cannot be a right way to own anyone, and there cannot be a kind and gentle way to steal from another, even if it involves no harm.

I remember reading about a farmer who took exceptionally good care of his animals. He even put on gentle music for them and talked to them every day. Even when the time came to kill the animals, soft music would be playing in the background, and he would speak soothing words of comfort to them. And then a quick and painless death you think, right? Wrong. No death is quick and painless, and even if there was such a thing, causing death to another being is never a good thing.

> "It's like you innately know, this is not right. Otherwise, I wouldn't feel so bad about it. I wouldn't feel so sad. And if it was righteous, if it was a truly good thing, then it would be a joyful thing. But I've never known anybody, who slaughters animals and finds it is a joyful thing."[2]
>
> **Harold Brown,** Former animal farmer

Even if by some miracle, other beings gave us their eggs, honey or their wool, it would not be appropriate to use them. If we were given a chance to speak to animals, what do you think they would say to us? I know, because I have experienced it. I can tell you that they plead with us. As they approach death, they jerk and squirm trying to free themselves. Some, too battered and worn out from the exhaustion of animal farming, eventually either die on the way to slaughter or just wait patiently until their lives end.

Even our pets are treated as property. Again, dogs go to the washroom when we tell them; they eat when we say, and we take them for walks when we deem so. They are working on our terms, on our schedule. When we go out, they are home alone, sometimes for many hours. In summer when we take them to the grocery store, they sit in the hot car. We view them as property because that is all nonhuman animals mean to us. Because animals are indifferent, and we believe we are top of the food chain, we can do as we please with them. Even vegans see pets as property. They are furry and cute so let's adopt/rescue one. Many vegans feed their rescued animal(s), other dead animals. In fact, for one animal saved, it means the suffering and death of thousands of animals. Thus, these vegans do more harm by paying people to kill many thousands of animals to feed to their companion animal(s). Even if we fed our pets strictly vegan foods, it sends a message to other people that it is okay to own and have pets. Again it sends a message to others that we can dominate other living beings and do with them as we please. This is morally unjustifiable. We should see to it that we don't support the animal industry at all, by not having pets. If we get people to stop eating animal foods and stop seeing them as property, then they will also stop using them for other reasons as well. Until we understand that animals are not here for us and that we shouldn't even use them, nothing will get better on this planet.

Bearing Witness

The truck approached the lights, and it stopped right in front of me. I was standing on a boulevard, bearing witness with many activists. In the truck were many pigs, crammed in very tightly, with scratches and bruises on them, some even standing on one another. As I was moving closer to the truck, one pig caught my attention. Our eyes met, and I saw fear, loneliness, and depression in that being. As we looked at each other, he/she asked me, "Why are you doing this to us?" At that moment, my heart sank, and I felt the lowest in all my life. With my head down, ashamed of what I had supported for decades, shedding tears, I replied, "I don't know."

In all my years of living on this planet, I was confronted with a deeply emotional experience that I will never forget. For the first twenty-six years of my life, I was unaware and unconscious of the harm and death that I was causing to innocent beings. That pig I interacted with that day just wanted to be free. He/she wanted to experience life, raising young and having a family, and frolicking in the meadows with other animals. But instead, we deny all of this and put them in cages in the stinking sheds of horror, only for them to later experience more fear, with knives gashing at their throats or bullets to their head.

I made a solemn promise to all the animals that I would do what I could to awaken humanity, to see that one day there would be no injustice and that we would all be free. I know the day will come when we all frolic in the meadows together and hug and cuddle with one another. A world where none of us are afraid, where we can live out our days in peace and freedom. That day is now.

4

We Can Live with Love

. . . .

Today we can live with love. We don't need to continue with the status quo, but instead, feel the love in our hearts. All we have to do is love every creature, by ceasing to eat animals, wearing them, testing on them, and using them for entertainment or anything else. It is that simple. We have no time to wait, no excuses. We are the ones who have to get up and make a stand. No one can do it for us. Only we can. No, governments can't do it for us and we cannot wait for tomorrow. Because tomorrow may never arrive. We are at the precipice, and everyone is jumping. Will we take the leap with them or take life into our own hands? The choice is ours, and only we can make the decision. We are the ones who need to use the power of love. Love is powerful. It heals all the suffering, all the violence, and it sheds all tears. The only tears we will experience, are from the tremendous joy and ecstasy gushing from our hearts.

The choices we make today shape the world we live in tomorrow. We want the best for the future for our children and grandchildren, and we want to grow up in a world of love and compassion, where everyone has equal opportunities in life. We all want to be free, with clean water, wholesome food, and a place to live. We all want a world in which we can go outside and not be afraid of anyone around us. A world where there are no locks, theft or violence of any kind. We need a world where we can all trust one another. No more racism, hate, sexism, homophobia, transphobia, and speciesism. We don't need to live in a capitalist, money grubbing society, where the rich get richer, but rather in a world where everyone shares and loves and there is no competition against one another. No more slaves and inequality of any kind. We need the world where everyone is free and accepted. Where we can go where we please, do as we please, and stay wherever we, please. No country borders, no passports, no paperwork, no taxes, and no armies. This world I am envisioning is possible.

5

Can We Cope in This Crazy World?

. . . .

In a crazy world such as ours, with a lack of love, humans have to cope somehow. We work in jobs that are mundane and non-fulfilling. We come home after a long day, only to be exhausted. We have no energy to cook up a wholesome meal, so we resort to fast food or microwavable dinners full of animal corpses. Because our bodies crave carbohydrates, later, we resort to eating fatty, salty bags of chips or sugary candies that make us feel even worse. We do all this while watching TV, and then we go to sleep. Many of us can't sleep due to indigestion or heartburn, so we medicate ourselves taking sleeping pills that leave us feeling groggy in the morning. Humans then combat this by drinking coffee, energy drinks or colas, and the whole routine starts all over again.

Working in a job, five, six, or even seven days a week, many tens of hours, only brings about sickness and depression. To combat this, people turn to buying all sorts of electronic gadgets, fancy vehicles, and large houses. These things do not make us truly happy. On weekends, some people end up going out with friends drinking (alcohol), which again wreaks havoc on the body. Then, joined by their friends, they mainly discuss their boring lives and mundane jobs.

This life only brings more unhappiness, depression and illness, eventually paving the way for diseases to arise. People then go to psychiatrists, taking medication after medication, until one day they drop dead of a heart attack or yield to cancer.

These people feel lost in their lives. They have come to the conclusion that there is no meaning to life, and so a lot of them give up altogether. Suicide rates are skyrocketing. Theft, murders, and rape are ever-more frequent. As a result, more jails are built, thus, more law enforcements are needed.

Not only this. People reinforce violence in their lives through the movies, television (mass-media news), books and magazines, video games, and the internet. Then they support such dogmas as institutionalized (organized) religions, political and educational systems, the military, and the pharmaceutical-medical complex. At the same time, they are all competing; trying to get ahead of everyone else.

What a crazy world we live in. During the festive seasons, like Thanksgiving, Christmas, and Hanukkah, again, dead animal corpses are at the centre of the traditions. These barbaric customs only reinforce the idea of domination of the innocent; a hierarchical nonsense, that leads to more illness, suffering, and death.

Instead, we should be non-conformists, drifting away from rituals and institutions. However, if we still do participate in holidays, like Christmas for example, don't buy into the materialism of it, by giving presents. And if we still decide to contribute to gifts, give people used items we no longer use, buy them a book or film they can learn from, or give them delicious vegan foods that can transition them to healthier eating.

We should be celebrating the joys and wonders of everyday life. Do something to make the world a better place. Be happy and play out in the fresh air. Go to a sanctuary and visit the animals. Go and visit friends and enjoy their company. Sing, dance, and have a party. That is what life is about: having fun. It is not about jobs where we work forty plus hours a week, to purchase expensive cars and large houses. It is about contributing to the fabric of life, by loving, being joyful, and happy.

Humans created violence. Now to create peace, all we need to do is remove the violence and start loving every being. That is it. Why is this task so simple, yet only a few people embrace it? Why is the world still in such chaos?

One theory is that it is our human nature not to want to change. Change for us takes a long time; millennia. And so we stick to our old habits and continue with the paradigm, following everyone else. We feel safe in large numbers. We don't like being the lone wolf. Waking up to an alarm and going off to a job we don't enjoy; we could not imagine not doing these things. "Eat a pizza without cheese on it? Are you ridiculous man!?" When we get stuck in a routine for a long period of our lives, and it becomes a habitual activity, then it is as if we are programmed. It's like a mental addiction.

When we look at addictions, it is not what the person is addicted to that is the only problem, it is the environment that person is in and the people closest to them. For someone's life to drastically improve, they need to turn their lives completely around. If they are in a mundane job and working long hours with not enough sleep and poor quality food and it goes on day after day, for years, their life is the problem. It is not necessarily only the foods they are eating, though, that is probably the biggest part of it. They need to examine their whole lifestyle.

If people cannot believe they can live another way and turn their lives around for the better, it is because they have not loved themselves. And I don't mean, "yes I like myself", and that is it. I mean deeply loving ourselves every day and every moment of our lives like we honestly mean it. Again change is hard. But how can someone break an addiction? I think it first starts with love. First, one has to love themselves, and then they will begin to love others. Once people start loving themselves, their consciousness awakens and their lives transform for the better. I am not exactly sure how, but again let the universe take care of that. How do we begin to love ourselves? If you would like to learn more, I highly suggest reading *Love Yourself Like Your Life Depends On It* by Kamal Ravikant.[1]

6
Unconscious Spirituality

· ·

When I was a child, I always loved animals. I had companion dogs and cats, and it was a blessing every time I played, ran, and cuddled with them.

People do not understand the repercussions of eating animals and their secretions. The fear, terror, and loneliness that the animals feel do not suddenly vanish into thin air once they die. Chefs understand this, and that is why when they prepare animal foods, they need the animals to be killed in a particular way so that the flesh is not tainted. Again, everything has energy vibrations. Energy is in all humans, and other animals as well, as we are manifested from the same energy source. When one consumes animal foods, no matter how the animals were treated, the vibrations of fear, depression, loneliness, and suffering from that dead animal is transferred to our bodies as the same apprehension, loneliness, and pain. It cannot be argued. What I am telling you is the truth. If you feel uncomfortable, tough. A lot of people feel nervous when vegans tell them where their food came from and how the animals were killed. And because of this, they either try to change the subject, leave the room or start to justify their actions like it causes no harm.

But there is no excuse for violence at all. Using animals is violence. Even giving them names and treating them as one of the family members, only at a later time to slash their throats, is violence. Violence only begets violence. At first, violence may feel good, but it always comes back to haunt us in bigger ways.

Because I ate large quantities of animal products, especially cheese, and eggs, I contained the vibrations of the animals experiences: all the fear and violence within me. And thus, I took out the anger on my companion animals, beating, kicking, and punching them. The reason all omnivores do not abuse companion animals is simple. Not everyone is going to abuse someone, just like, not everyone is going to steal from someone, or rob a bank or become a slaughterhouse worker. Everyone has a karmic reaction that is destined for them. And everyone's karma is different. Whatever the action, it has a reaction that is sent out to the cosmos which eventually comes back to us. For most people it is disease and illness (inner). And for others, it is some form of mental sickness (external), as in millions of cases of animal, spousal or child abuse.

Some people will never make the connection when it comes to animal foods and the harm it causes. All the violence experienced on this planet is the result of what we do to animals for food. But because people, even vegetarians, are blinded by external events, they do not realize that animal agriculture is the problem and that everything stems from herding animals. Take the case of mentally disabled children, for example, they are born with this defect usually because of what their mothers ate when they were in her womb. Fish, because of the high mercury content is a big key factor in this.[1]

Think about this for a moment. In hospitals right now, how many people are ill or on the verge of dying? Even though the vegan population is still relatively small, I will guess ninety-nine percent of the people who end up in hospitals are omnivores either waiting to be hacked to pieces or given some drugs. And how many vegans do you know who cause intentional violence to others? I don't know anyone who does, and I know a lot of vegans. Even, the Animal Liberation Front (ALF), involved in direct action of freeing animals from laboratories and farms and cause destruction to corporate property, have not killed a single human or nonhuman being. All the wars that are raging and all the poisons of the Earth are caused by those who consume animal foods.

Maybe you don't know any vegans, but my point is, that vegans have never caused harm to another being. You will notice that they are loving and caring people, trying to cause the least harm. And yes, I understand there are the rare few vegans who cause deliberate violence and property damage or believe that all humans should die, but this number is less than one percent of the vegan population. When we look at the omnivore population that cause harm and suffering, 100 percent of them do. All I am saying is that throughout history, all of the violence is caused by omnivores. Vegans will never cause deliberate harm to another.

Respect for all sentient beings is at the core of veganism. Love and kindness and compassion are essential, but they are doled out arbitrarily by humans - whereas respect is a basic, core ethic that is all-inclusive. As vegans, we want to see a world of love and joy, where people are celebrating, cooperating, and playing with one another. We don't like violence, and so we don't cause it, or, at least, we try to avoid it whenever possible.

It is also worth mentioning, that as vegans, it is upsetting to communicate, or even be in the same room with many non-vegans, as the conversations and foods are that of violence. That is why when vegans celebrate holidays and have other gatherings, they usually prefer to socialize exclusively with other vegans. It is not that we don't like other people, for sure we love humans. It is only because as vegans we want to be able to share things in common with fellow vegans. Because most vegans do not have much in common with non-vegans, we tend to disassociate with them during the holidays.

When omnivores get together with one another, it is usually over food or drinks and, usually something containing the violence of eggs, dairy or flesh of animals. We don't like being around these foods or the negative vibrations, and so we stay as far away from them as possible. When vegans celebrate life, they want as little as possible to do with negativity and violence. Our world reinforces negativity like it is a good thing. It is not.

Also worth noting, is the dull omnivore

conversations at these gatherings. People usually complain about their lives, illnesses, work-related issues or whatever celebrity buzz or tragic news is currently trending. All which further reinforce negativity and violence. These discussions are never enlightening. They never seem to help the world in any way and are utterly nonsensical. As vegans, we do not want to be a part of it. Though vegans do not always share deep thoughts of spirituality and consciousness, when we celebrate life, it is all about the positive aspects of life, celebration, and love. While yes, we understand there is much suffering in the world, when we celebrate life with friends, we focus on positivity, the joys, and happiness of life. A celebration is supposed to be about loving, sharing, caring, joy, and happiness. Not about harm, suffering, violence, negativity, and unhappiness. But whenever I go to non-vegan gatherings, it usually seems that way.

In a world that is not yet vegan, vegans are challenged every day to find situations and environments that perfectly align with our ethical stance and values. Unfortunately, there are times when we must shop at supermarkets or eat out at restaurants that sell and serve animal foods. And in the process, seeing products, the production of which has caused extreme suffering and violence. But we don't want our lives filled with violence, and so we try avoiding these places whenever possible. It doesn't mean we flee from situations of suffering or death, but we may pray and meditate in given circumstances. When it comes to traditions like gatherings and celebrations, which are supposed to be a time for love and joy, as vegans, we don't want to surround ourselves with all the violence and negativity, and so, again, we try avoiding these places whenever possible.

However, as vegans, we understand that to create an Eden world, we need to educate others. We are not hermits, and therefore, whenever we get a chance we spread the message of love and compassion to the world.

Our lives are not perfect, yet we have to strive to do our best. Sometimes that might mean we need to be witnesses to extreme violence or be ridiculed by others. But we have to be strong and continue loving those who are unawakened. It takes the spiritual masters and the enlightened ones to make a difference.

In all my years on this planet, I have never been so blessed since I became a vegan. Being vegan has brought me more pleasures, truths, and knowledge than in the first twenty-six years of my life. I am not proud that it took such a long time to awaken or that I abused animals and supported a system of the utmost cruelty. But I am glad that at least I did awaken, and experienced what I have. I don't think I was even truly living when I was an omnivore. What I know today I cannot erase. I cannot undo the knowledge that has permeated my heart and mind.

It is this fabrication of love, the experience, and knowledge that has led me to my life I live today. I am a changed person, and I am thankful for whom I have become. Of course, my life is not perfect, and there are still trials and tribulations to contend to. But as I continue a life of love and joy, I know situations will improve.

I now notice and appreciate the beauty of all aspects of life. I look upon a leaf, tree, river, squirrel, and ant, with love and contentment. I know that I am now a part of the universal order of the woven fabric of life, here to make a difference for the greater good of every creature and the environment. We each are not a speck of dust in the universe, but rather; the universe itself. We are a big part of this intricate existence. I feel every drop of my love pouring out to the world. And as that happens, it transforms the experience into something more magnificent than it already is.

After decades of being asleep, unaware of true spiritual reality, I finally left home. I left my cultural beliefs and traditions for something greater and more benevolent. I understood that this was my path in life and that I wanted to be a part of the greater good of the universe. Nature taught me not to use and harm, but to love and care. Animals taught me to be their voice and spread compassion to others.

My family, my culture and all that I grew up with, did not teach me one useful thing about spiritual existence. I awakened on my own, through the glowing wisdom of love within my heart. As a young child, unfortunately, programmed by every institution in my culture, I only learned to be violent. It was not until I started questioning the essential teachings of our society did I finally begin to question my behaviors.

In my late teens is when I started the practice of "self-inquiry meditation" into the mind and heart of who I was. I would question everything, including human-caused suffering and violence. Strangely enough, I was the one causing misery. I couldn't make the connection, as the love was hidden and suppressed in me for many years. One day, after looking at an older photo of myself, taken at the circus, - where I was sitting next to a bear wearing a muzzle, - I realized that we were violent to other animals. Though that still did not awaken me. I thought the problem was something in the outer world. What I didn't realize was that the problem was me. As time went on, something within my psyche triggered an awakening, and I stopped eating the flesh and secretions of animals altogether.

We can't seem to wrap our heads around the fact that none of our physical issues are ever external. We are the problem; each and every one of us. We don't want to take the blame, and tend to condemn others for all of our problems. We create our lives: all the situations, and events. Thus, we have a choice to either create a beautiful life for ourselves or a miserable one. That is why some people are always happy, while others are mostly unhappy.

People who are considerably unhappy, usually blame others for their mistakes. But they should examine their own lives and not the lives of others. They should not judge and criticize others, but rather, they should take responsibility for their own life. Every person is a free-thinker with the ability to make individual decisions. In every moment, we can make choices; either for the better or worse. It's as if we are the scriptwriters, and we decide what goes in and what doesn't. We can either choose to live a perfect life or blame and judge others.

Because of the cultural indoctrination, I was unaware of the violence I was causing to others. As I got older - in my mid to late teens - I started becoming more aware of the harm I was causing. And I recognized that I was the one who was violent, but that still didn't stop me from hurting animals. Remembering those times is painful, but I think that sharing my story with people, has helped me deal with the bad memories. I realize it was immoral because my heart bled and I cried every time I attacked my companion animals. Then why did I continue abusing them? I have come to understand that, because I was consuming the vibrations of the terrified animals, that those violent vibrations came out in my actions. The farmers and slaughterhouse workers did to the farm animals what I did to my companions. Though I never killed any of my pets, I did abuse them terribly.

As I look back at that time, I can't believe the things I've done. But, like almost everyone who abuses animals, I did not understand what I was doing. We think we do, but everything we do comes from being unaware. And we follow our culture because everyone does, so it must be the right thing to do. Because millions of others do the same thing should we as well?

If many people start eating feces, does that means we should too? People would probably call me crazy for saying such things, but if we were taught that feces gave us protein, calcium or extra B12 or that it was a natural thing to do, we would be eating excrement or jumping off bridges.

This reminds me of a saying I once heard, about walking behind and following the heard [of asses]. In the literal sense, we are a bunch of asses, though of course I do not like to make fun of donkeys. Because donkeys are probably smarter and more intelligent than we are. Would they jump off a bridge after so many other donkeys? I think not.

The years go by and suddenly we are fifty. As we complain about our past and the terrible life we had, we keep blaming it on our children, our parents or our siblings. The past though, does not exist. No point in fretting over something that is nothing but a memory. The future isn't here either, so don't worry about it. Yes, we can definitely plan for the future, but don't fuss over things that are not here. Just worry about the present and enjoy the moment. This is what spiritual masters talk about: to be mindful in the present.

Most people do not know how to be mindful in the moment. Our thoughts are always racing, and we are busy running place to place. We need to love, and be love, at every awakened moment. Very few of us are awake and unconditionally loving. To be mindful in the present moment, is simply to love and respect all beings. When humans become more conscious, there arises an awareness of the terrible suffering caused by the torture and killing of animals for their flesh and secretions.

It comes down to consciously experiencing the now, with full unconditional love for all who lives. When we look at a river or tree, a deep appreciation and love for them is felt. Because they give us life, and they supply many other creatures with the chance to experience this earthly beauty. This is what is meant to live.

We also need to be mindful about what we eat, and the harm and suffering each morsel of food causes. And turn it around, so that we do not cause any violence. Love is there; it is the healer and ultimate guide to awakening. It cannot be destroyed; it even heals hate, violence, and suffering. And that is why we never retaliate, and use violence to fight violence, but rather turn to love for healing.

When we look at the existence of life, nothing is separate. There are not even internal or external powers. There are no humans or trees, no rocks or mountains. It is all energy in various forms. It is pure energy that causes everything to occur, even when speaking and breathing. It is so because everything is one. All life originated from one source, one big bang or one god, the universal life energy. How did that come to be? No one knows. That is the mystery of life.

Even when I mention a human, an animal or nature, these may not even exist. They only exist in the external present what we perceive to be real. But they may not be real. It does not mean that even if nothing exists, that we can cause deliberate harm. No, because our being does not want to carry out those actions, as they are not vibrations of love. Spiritual beings such as humans are receptive only to love.

The universe is like a movie; there is a blank screen, and we are the writers and the filmmakers. We can create any life we please, understanding of course, that there are natural laws set in place. Who governs these sets of laws? It is not a person or a book, as a lot of religious believers have come to understand. These morals stem from our hearts. Therefore, objective morality and truth are instinctive to our being. It is part of the natural laws.

7
Natural Laws

. . . .

Natural Laws are a set of rights or values that are governed by nature and the universe, rather than by rules of society. Natural Laws are binding in that they are immutable. They can never be changed and are never based on belief systems. Natural Laws are inherent, existing truths, having a solid foundation in nature. These principles always work, they do not care who the being is, or if they understand the law or not. It works every time and in every case, even if they are innocent or ignorant. Therefore, we must understand these principles.

Man did not create such laws, so it is, in effect, internal. If we believe it is humans that make these laws, we are unbelievably mistaken. It is the creator of the universe that puts these laws into effect. Like it or not, these laws are in affect whether you agree or disagree with them. It is like the law of gravity. It is universally understood that if one jumps off a cliff, the reality of gravity will ensure injury or death. Yes, you can break Natural Laws, but you cannot break them without negative consequences.[1, 2]

The Principle of **Mentalism**
The Principle of **Interconnectedness**
The Principle of **Vibration**
The Principle of **Polarity**
The Principle of **Rhythm**
The Principle of **Cause and Effect**
The Principle of **Gender**
The Principle of **Love**

Mentalism

Everything in creation is a manifestation of mind. Which means, everything that has been created, has to have been made by a thought that proceeded it. Thoughts lead to a manifestation of things and events. Thoughts create our state of existence and quality of life.

Interconnectedness

This law is called 'correspondence', which I like to call 'interconnectedness'. The universe is contained within the individual, and the individual is also contained within the universe. They are reflections of each other. These two entities cannot be separated from one another. When we learn the structure of one, we learn the formation of the other and vice versa. I would like to reiterate, that all things on this planet are interconnected. Nothing is separate, even in the material world. Everything happens for a reason, and that is because our thoughts, actions, and emotions create the outcome and situation. We came from one source, and thus, we only perceive things to be separate because our eyes see everything as an illusion. However, in this true spiritual reality, we are all one.

Vibration

Nothing rests, and therefore, there is always motion in every living thing and sentient being. There is even vibrational motion in inanimate objects, like a desk. And therefore, everything contains vibrational energy that is consistently in motion.

That is why, whenever we consume food, it causes either a negative or positive vibration. When we eat the fear, suffering, and death in animal foods, we transfer those same emotions into our heart, body, and mind. They do not suddenly vanish into thin air. It is very similar to electricity. Energy is both in the cable and outlet. When the cable is plugged into the terminal, the energy vibrations from both the cable and the outlet interact with each other. Power (energy) from the cable or the outlet doesn't suddenly vanish into thin air. They move in a back and forth motion between themselves. This is how a vacuum and hair dryer work. And that is how humans operate within the universal energy-field and how energy vibrations work within all things. It is precisely like the cable and outlet. For example, the cable can be described as the person; the outlet is the animal, and the power generator is the farmer and slaughterhouse worker. They work together even before one's lips have touched the flesh or secretion of the animal.

And even though inanimate objects contain moving energy, it doesn't mean it is the same as the life-force energy within a human, a dog, pig or fish. These sentient beings have automatic sensory systems that make them different to non-moving objects, in that they can suffer and feel pain while a table or lamp do not possess these sensations.

Polarity

Everything has a dual nature to it. There are polarities in everything that exists. Everything has poles, and everything has its pairs of opposites. May I remind you of good versus evil, right from wrong, lightness versus darkness, and masculine and feminine.

Rhythm

Everything has a rhythm to it. All things rise and fall, and everything flows, like a tide, in and out. It has a tendency for something to swing in a certain way.

Cause and Effect

Any action, thought or emotion that we send out causes an effect. If one consumes animal foods, they directly cause an effect of that action. The effect may not occur immediately, as there is a time-lag between the cause and the effect. That is why many people who cause harm unconsciously, do not connect the harm to the cause. If every time they were stung by a bee when they caused suffering, they would eventually stop causing the harm. But because there is a time gap they cannot make that link. At some future point in time, the law of the universe will manifest the consequence of what we generated by setting that cause into motion.

Gender

Gender - masculine, and feminine - principles exist in everything. In the mind, mental gender is the co-existence of the masculine and feminine aspects of the human mind, and when they both co-exist with each other, there is a balance of harmony within the being, which can trigger love within the heart. Though some people consider themselves gender-neutral when it comes to their sex, they too even have masculine and feminine sides to them.

Love

There is an eighth principle, which encompasses all these laws. There are various names for it, but not many people know about it, as it is considered the lost law. This law I call "Love". Because again, love heals everything. And so, the principle of love has to be embraced first.

Love is at the heart. It is the solution to the world's problems. However, love by itself without acknowledging and understanding the rest of the Natural Laws has no meaning by itself. Yes, I could have said "love", and that was it. But love by itself without any explanation, means nothing.

What does love truly mean? To us, it means that we love our friends, family, spouses, and our dog or cat. But the love ends there. Our circle of compassion only includes those who are closest to us. The definition of love is watered down; it has lost its real meaning. Most dictionaries will describe it applying to humans only. Love is a feeling of strong affection for all life – both to humans and nonhuman animals and to nature. It must also include the world as a whole, the universe, other galaxies and planets and other species not on this planet. If we exclude anyone from our moral consideration, are we, therefore, actually embracing love?

Language is funny, especially the English language. There are a lot of words that mean many different things. If I say "I love you" to my spouse, it means one thing. It means that I have a deep affection for my other and sincerely feel some emotions for that person. When I say "I love you mom" or "I love you brother," it is not the same type of love as in the previous example. The same word now has two different meanings. And this can get a little confusing at times.

8
The Meaning of Life

. . . .

The universe is infinitely massive, and because so, it is hard to fathom the meaning of life. It is like a painting; we cannot absorb the whole painting in only a few moments. There are some who study artwork for hours upon hours, and even year after year, and look at the finest details. They stand at it from far and then they come closer to observe it. They take it to curators to examine it. And still the viewer is in awe of the painting. There is something that they still miss. It is similar when I write a book or an article; I go over it many times. And every time there is something that needs correcting or something to add or remove. There is something overlooked, both in the painting as well as the written piece. Some of the most famous paintings and books have written codes or messages hidden within them. And that is why people continuously examine them time and time again.

And so the universe is something like a painting. We examine it, and there are hidden messages and meanings behind them. And we analyze every part of our existence. That is what consciousness is. That is what it means to be mindful at every moment. So what is the meaning of life? A lot of people believe that there is no meaning to life.

As Shaun Monson puts it in his audiobook *Unity*, "After all, what is the meaning of life, if not to raise our level of consciousness?"[1] That could be it. Many spiritual masters have come to the conclusion that "Non-violence" and "Unconditional love", are the meaning of life. I can't argue with them either.

We still ponder the question and the complex reality of existence, "What is the meaning of life?" If that question were put to a scientist, carpenter, and a Buddhist monk, they would each probably give a different response. Maybe they are all correct, or maybe they are all dead wrong because we do not know. We are still expanding our knowledge and further raising our consciousness. Perhaps we will never know, and never come to the understanding of the existence and meaning of life itself.

I have come to the understanding from many years of meditation, that we are here on this planet to experience love and happiness. We are here to learn and grow, working in harmony with the earth and one another. Our presence is to be mindful in the now.

As I search deep into my heart, I realize that there is no answer to the meaning of life. We have our thoughts of what that might be. But maybe there is no meaning to this existence. In that case, can we cause violence and crime and do as we please? If our actions have no effect on anyone, can we rob banks, steal, and eat anything we please?

As I wonder about these things, it deeply depresses

me. What if life does not exist, if there is no meaning to life or if we do not even exist in the physical realm? Then, would there be a reason to live? As I am walking in the snow, I question, am I even seeing snow? Or am I living in a tropical paradise and do not even know it?

These questions have baffled some of the greatest minds. But people cannot even start to examine these things, if we still enslave, torture, and murder other living beings. This is the turning point of our human intelligence and evolution. Because we all have blinders on and don't want to seek the truth; which is love, we cannot progress to a higher state of consciousness. If our vibratory energy levels are very low, we certainly cannot advance beyond that spiritual level. If we perceive the current reality as normal and this is all that life has to offer, will we ever be happy? Is it normal, natural, and necessary to be using and killing animals for food, when clearly in today's world there is no need for such violence? In the external world, which we are all a part of, our eyes believe everything to be real. We are fed all sorts of nonsense through the mainstream media: television, radio, and newspapers, even movies. And also of course from organized religion, the pharmaceutical industry, educational, and political systems. Then do we ever wonder why our world is in such chaos? Humanity is on the brink of collapse. Do you think these institutions are doing anything to solve any of our problems? No. In fact, they do the opposite. They are here to enslave and keep us in bondage. If an organization or institution is part of the dominating culture of herding animals, they can never be part of the solution.

They are numbing us down. Like robots, we take orders. Like sheep, we follow the herd. It is not a pleasing sight: seeing animals, one after another, going to their deaths. But this is what is happening to us as well. Humans too are being led to their deaths, by way of poor choices that lead to hospitals and cemeteries.

And again, we don't do anything about it, because of stupid excuses and justifications. Maybe we're too lazy to change, or it is an inconvenience when we go out to social gatherings, or we couldn't care less. But hey, enough with the petty little excuses! The animals don't want to hear them, neither does Mother Earth.

And so it comes down to the ego. Until we face our ego and embrace love, nothing will ever change for the better. We cannot expect to live in a world of love, compassion, and peace until we change our habits. Our hearts are falling apart, and the only way to create change in this world is first to change ourselves, then to educate others. Change is hard, I know. I was living the life that every omnivore does. I was unaware of the violence I was causing to innocent beings. Stop being a caveman/cavewoman. Start being an intelligent human who cares about others, and who devotes their time to making this world a better place for all.

Turn off the TV and cease watching mainstream news. Remove the violent movies and video games. Start making a real difference in this world. Stop supporting such dogmas as organized religions, educational systems, and politics. We have an obligation to do so. Start eating healthier plant-based meals, including a large portion of raw fresh fruits and veggies. High-fat, greasy animal foods are taking us to the operating room. Our kitchens are now the largest scientific experimenting labs, filled with pills, powders, potions, and dead bodies and secretions of animals. No more do we live amongst the orchards and gardens, but instead right in the midst of a morgue and cemetery.

Go out and experience the beauty of nature. Go for long hikes and bicycle rides. See the world, go backpacking to other countries, help volunteer at animal sanctuaries, become an activist; be a voice for the voiceless. Do it. We have no time to lose.

9

The Beauty of Mother Earth

. . . .

Surrounded by nature, I sat and gazed at the river. What magnificent beauty. I am grateful to be alive to experience it. I had fallen for the splendor of nature. As I stood there in quiet contemplation listening to the sounds, feeling in awe of the surroundings and serene music of the brook, I was in love with Mother Earth. It was a cold day, and all the animals were probably in their warm homes with their families, enjoying each other's love. It is sad that I do not see as many animals in nature as I once did. I remember feeding seeds to birds, and peanuts to chipmunks. What a joyous time that was. I even fell asleep once, only to awaken to many animals around me.

That is what the natural world is: beautiful, benevolent, magnificent, and breathtaking. We see many animals working in harmony with one another, sharing, and frolicking. We see nature supplying the food and the oxygen, for life to survive. We witness microorganisms and tiny insects in the soil, working to create a symbiosis so others can live. Then there are the few people who cultivate and plant orchards and tend gardens, paving the way for a brighter future and better tomorrow.

Nature provides all the food for everyone to enjoy.

The sun is bright, dazzling, and warm. We are looking to the sun for warmth, plucking the fruits of the earth for our nutriment. Looking at grass, for example, I have a deep appreciation for it. As I sit on the ground and feel the grass between my fingers and palms, I soak up the sun's rays. The air is pure, sounds coming from all corners of the forest. I am so blessed to be here to experience such utopia. I love my life, I love nature, and have a deep affinity for all that lives.

Such an experience is not that uncommon when we become love. We start experiencing more of the beauty and splendour around us. Once we start appreciating the littlest aspects of life, like the grass, a branch or the crawling of a caterpillar, our consciousness begins to expand.

Beside me is an evergreen tree. Never have I been thankful for the ability to be in such presence of an abundant life and world. Gently I caress the tree, feeling the roughness of the texture. I love the majestic, dark green colour. I then head back along the river. Even though it is a frigid day in the middle of winter, I love and appreciate the place I am at. I thank the universe for bringing me into this world, and for letting me experience such wonders of the earth.

In any other time in history, I might have been a slave, or ridiculed or even jailed for expressing my ideas, or born into unfortunate circumstances and environment. Though my life is not perfect, I am greatly fortunate for being able to live and experience the life I am in, where it is relatively safe to go outside and walk about, wherever I please. The universe has given me this rich life, a life that has opened me up to new possibilities and a new way of regarding the world and the opportunity to do with my life. I am so blessed. Every day I express my gratitude; thanking the universe for this holy life. Thank you. Thank you. Thank you. Thank you for giving me this life, and thank you for taking me on this spiritual journey of a blissful experience of life on this planet.

Even though we may be dissatisfied with our lives, or wish we were somewhere else, we need to be appreciative and thankful for our current situation. Millions of people would do anything to be where we are today. If we have water, food, shelter, and our health we are the most fortunate ones on earth. Some people have no chance of progressing with their lives. That is one of the reasons why I became vegan, so I could help feed a hungry world and not support wars and violence. Veganism does solve all of the problems. No doubt about it.

It is a shame, though; many people do not see the beauty on our planet. Instead, their lives are nothing but violence. And strangely, they view their lives as normal. They go to their jobs, and they think it's normal. They drink coffee several times a day to combat sleepiness, and they believe it's normal. They watch the six o'clock news, the TV blaring with tragic news and death, and they think it's reality. People consume animal food, only to later take medications and supplements, and they believe it's normal. They follow indoctrinations and beliefs like churches and The Bible blindly, thinking that this is going to create peace. These people are misled and programmed to believe falsehoods. What they never do is figure out things for themselves.

People follow everyone blindly, without ever questioning any of it. They believe normalcy to be a part of everyday life. I know that one day we will reach the truth about the existence of life within the cosmos. We need to raise our consciousness and stop being materialistic, money grabbers, taking what we think is rightfully ours. Being instead benevolent creators, saviours, and guardians of this earth; sharing and co-creating life on this planet.

And when we get to higher planes of consciousness, then will we be able to comprehend if extraterrestrial life-forms exist on other planets and galaxies. And maybe, just maybe, they would be interested in contacting us. But the whole idea of encountering extraterrestrial life forms is utterly inconceivable if we are still part of the dominant culture of the herding society. With our low vibrational energy level, we are practically un-evolved, and could not fathom aliens from other galaxies. When it comes to violence, I don't think any other species are more violent than we are. How much crueler can we become when it comes to enslaving, torturing, and slaughtering other beings?

10
Awakening

. . . .

So how does one awaken to love? Unfortunately, no one can just awaken at the snap of a finger. It has to be done when the mind and heart connect to love. But one cannot just make it happen, it occurs spontaneously at some later time.

Before anything can start, the mind has to be in a deep spiritual meditative state, and the heart has to be all loving not wanting to cause any suffering. When the mind is aligned with that notion of not wanting to use or cause harm to another living creature, then the mind and heart, work simultaneously with each other for the awakening process to begin. Again, no one can instigate the awakening process when they want to. It comes about spontaneously at the appropriate time. It might occur one year from now, ten years, fifty years, or it may never happen in one's lifetime.

For most people they are heavily conditioned by the culture that it is hard to get out of the trance. No matter how many hours of meditation or praying one accomplishes, this may never trigger a revelation. And so the solution is to start loving all creatures. This, however, is not easy, as our society indoctrinates us to eat a certain way and follow orders. The longer we have been conditioned for, the harder it is for us to free ourselves from the conditioning.

When we awaken to love, and become vegan, this is the first step on our journey. Many people bypass the awakening stage altogether and go directly to veganism. Let me explain.

First, we need to define the term vegan. The definition was put forth by Donald Watson, in 1944.

> "Veganism denotes a philosophy and way of living which seeks to exclude—as far as is possible and practicable—all forms of exploitation of, and cruelty to, animals for food, clothing, or any other purpose; and by extension, promotes the development and use of animal-free alternatives for the benefit of humans, animals, and the environment. In dietary terms it denotes the practice of dispensing with all products derived wholly or partly from animals."[1]
>
> **The Vegan Society, 1979, the Memorandum and Articles of Association**

As we read above, veganism means, "to be kind and compassionate towards animals." It also means "to refrain from cruelty to animals as much as possible for food, clothing or any other purpose." This is a great definition; however, it is not complete, as it misses a few points. Awhile back I wrote my own definition of veganism and still today I am updating and tweaking it.

> "Veganism is an ethical and spiritual philosophy and way of life, which causes the least harm on the planet and to every living being, and seeks not to use or kill animals for food, clothing, entertainment, testing or any other purpose. One must purchase or grow organic, preferably, veganic or wild cultivated produce whenever possible."
>
> **Michael Lanfield**, June 2016

When people bypass the awakening stage, they usually become vegan for selfish reasons; like their health or fitness. But the motivation for veganism, was kindness and compassion for animals. And so, I believe the reason most people go back to eating animal foods is because they didn't awaken to the ethical aspects of veganism in the first place. Without a real awakening, one cannot be vegan, because, as the original definition implies, veganism is a philosophy and way of living. It is not merely a diet. It is not even to help the environment. As the definition says, it, "…promotes the development and use of animal-free alternatives for the benefit of humans, animals, and the environment." So yes, veganism does help people and the environment, but that is not the primary motivation for veganism.

Unless people awaken to love and compassion for all beings and become vegan for ethical-spiritual reasons, almost certainly they will fall back to eating animal foods. That is why, statistically, nine out of ten vegans go back to flesh/secretion eating. They have to do it for the animals first and foremost to be truly vegan. They can't do it to impress anyone, or for their health or the environment. They can only do it for the love of animals. Though there are some who initially do it for their health, later realizing the ethical side of veganism, once again, most people go back to eating animals, if their motivation for staying vegan is not for ethical concerns. Some people ask me what is the difference between "vegetarian" and "vegan"? Here are basic diet definitions, in my own words.

Vegetarianism

Abstains from eating of all animal flesh (including chicken and fish), but includes dairy, eggs, and/or honey.

Veganism

Abstains from eating all animal foods, including meat (flesh), dairy, eggs, honey, and all ingredients derived from animals.

And those definitions are diet related only. Vegetarians may also use animals in other ways, like for entertainment, or testing and ingredients in products, for clothing or other means.

Eventually, once we awaken to the vegan way of living, we need to understand a few basic things to further our journey and not to fall off the wagon. There have been many books on how to deal with friends and family and how to transition to veganism, but by no means is this book designed to go into all the details. It is merely giving a basic outline and principles on what people should do as new vegans.

When you become vegan, go through the spiritual journey slowly. Do not progress too fast. That is how I almost fell on my face. I am glad someone told me. If you really care about animals, there is only one way to transition to veganism: The way to transition is to do it immediately cold tofu, by starting to eat vegan right away and throwing all your animal foods in your trash. Add in some vegan transitional foods, like meat analogues and dairy substitutes, while adding in whole staple foods like, fruit, vegetables, whole-grains, legumes, nuts, and seeds. I would highly recommend everyone add into their diet, a small portion of vegan transitional foods. This is so one can be sure, that they won't be tempted to eat non-vegan burgers and hotdogs, sausages, and cheese pizzas. Also, do not be tempted to eat non-vegan foods outside of your home.

There are many brands of vegan meat and dairy alternatives as well as alternatives to eggs and honey. Read my book *The Interconnectedness of Life* for more informational on vegan transitional foods.

It is crucial once you become vegan, as previously mentioned, to spread the message to others. People need to know what is going on, and education is always the best way to do it. First before you educate others, you need to have the necessary knowledge yourself.

The way it was for me, I organized a few demonstrations, got signs made, and some activists joined in. I also volunteered at other demonstrations and protests mainly holding signs and leafletting. In the period of one to three years, I educated myself by watching videos, documentaries, and reading books and articles. Eventually finding out what my purpose was, and I put my talent to use. I started writing articles and my first book, and also created websites and my YouTube channel. I also gave lectures, hosted film screenings; I did Pay Per Views, OVEDs (outdoor video educational displays) and organized large vegan expos.

Today my main forms of education are my writings, YouTube videos, occasional film work, and lectures and interviews. These days, I am still learning, educating myself and also meditating. I am highly spiritual, so I do a lot of connecting with nature. It is a fun journey, but I still have a lot to learn.

When it comes to friends and family, even as a vegan since 2009, this part is the most difficult for me. And it is hard, even for many other vegans as well. When I went vegan, I didn't have many friends to begin with, so I met new friends along the way. As for most people, they will still have non-vegan friends. One needs to do their best when it comes to educating them. Do not bombard friends with veganism all the time, but also, do not be quiet. Show them a few films here and there, make them vegan meals and take them to vegan restaurants. If some of their friends are not open-minded and do not respect their beliefs, dump those friends. They are not their truly good friends. Even if they do not become vegan (even after several years), don't worry. We are not here to change them. In fact, we can never change anyone, we can only change ourselves. So just plant the vegan seeds as best as we can and keep nurturing them every so often.

When it comes to our immediate family, this is where things get tricky. By no means am I an expert in this. I stay as far away as possible from my family, especially during festive seasons like Christmas. When it comes to my mom, she is more understanding and knowledgeable as she is mostly vegan. However, we still have the odd argument when we visit each other. All I can say in these circumstances, do our best and be compassionate, loving, and understanding towards them.

When it comes to gatherings and outings at one's workplace, or with family and friends, this is where it can get a little tricky. Today, I never bother going out anywhere, unless it is a purely vegan restaurant or to a supermarket or health store to pick up vegan food. But when I started out many years ago, it was difficult as I often got dragged to places that were not vegan and it was hard to watch others eat the corpses of dead animals and their secretions. It was disgusting. No more can I do that. I cannot sit near anyone who consumes animal foods.

When it comes to friends, I am lucky as virtually all

my friends are vegan. So we can go out to the same places and talk about the same things. Sometimes, I invite my family or neighbours to vegan outings. Again, if our friends care enough about us, they will accommodate us every time. They will go out of their way, to make us feel comfortable. Instead of eating at meat restaurants they will come with us to vegan restaurants. They will invite us to their place for a delicious vegan meal. However, if they are not accommodating, and they ridicule us all the time, they are not true friends.

11
A Vegan World

. . . .

Can you picture a vegan world? No, because it hasn't happened yet. This world is not now, but sometime in the distant future. Imagine this: the majority of the world is now vegan. We all hold the same vision. All sentient beings now feel safe, because no human wants to harm anyone else. We don't have to lock our doors, as we are not part of the violent, fear-based society. Everyone is our friend. We can talk to anyone as if we know them. We can go to the supermarket or a restaurant, and not have to worry about what to order or purchase, because everything is cruelty-free. There are also many veganic (no animal inputs) farms and greenhouses open all year-round where we can buy produce. More vegan transitional products are hitting the store shelves every day; food is ever more affordable than ever as Government subsidies are now being put into growing food rather than killing food. Governments now understand the issues and are helping the people by subsidizing local family farmers grow food and ethical family businesses. No more are we buying goods from manufacturers that employ slave workers, but rather from companies who only produce ethically made products.

It also makes us feel better when we help support local fair trade family businesses. Since most people eat vegan, grains and other food that farmed animals ate, are now going to feed the poor. People and companies are now very generous with their time that they help build houses for people in disadvantaged countries. And because the prices for plant foods have gone down drastically, everyone all over the world can now afford to buy nutritious food for their families.

In this future vegan world, people no longer have to beg for money on the street corner or steal. Instead, they earn a decent living doing what they love. You see, because veganism has made the world a better place, no one is depressed, and they do not have illnesses. Everyone is working in harmony with one another. Though the monetary currency is still used, more than ever, people are sharing and trading. And jobs are not like they once used to be.

Because most people don't see the sense in buying useless products they don't need, they work far less. Instead of working the regular forty-hour shift, most people work half the time or less, and a lot of them donate their time instead, volunteering. Most do it because of the love of it. Though they do get a very decent salary, in some pockets of the world, people only share and trade with one another. They work in cooperation and harmony.

So where do all the farmed animal go? Do people start releasing them to nature? Not exactly. As the demand for animal products goes down, so does the amount of animals that are killed. Other animals go on to sanctuaries and some, unfortunately, are still being slaughtered for those who can't give up their meat addiction. But those days are long gone, there are very few people who still eat animal foods. And the ones that do purchase their food are from the traditional backyard farmers or rear their own animals. More people are now eating less meat than they used to or have gone completely vegan.

No longer are jobs, media, and corporations the same. There are very few enterprises left; instead, small local shops surround local communities. Jobs are no longer the traditional jobs, but work people are proud of. People drive less, so they either take public transit or bike everywhere. Since most people buy fewer goods, they don't need as much money as they used to. Therefore there is not much need for work. Some people have even abandoned the traditional job altogether, living in close-knit intentional communities, sharing with one another. As there is more time in everyone's lives to do as we wish, people volunteer to help make this world a better place for everyone. As a society, we are now using alternative energy sources. In fact, electricity is now even more affordable than ever. In some parts of the world free living is becoming the norm, where people only share, care, and love one another.

How is this possible? When we forgo our old ways of living and adopt an entirely new loving way of life, then we won't be concerned about money, prestige, fame, wealth, and other ego concerns. The trouble with the past was that we let ego get in the way. What we considered normal yesterday is not normal today.

In this future vegan world, we will remember when slavery was abolished in all areas of the world: just as we will recall the former inequality now gone. Equality is here, and everyone is treated fairly. There was once a time when children worked as slaves, abducted from their families, in the cocoa industry in Ivory Coast. Today there is none of that as most people either purchase carob or fair trade cocoa, where everyone earns a decent living.

When it comes to the education system, no longer is it institutionalized, but rather independently run. The society we grew up in, is vastly different from now. It is being phased out for something called love. Schools today, instead, of being taught by teachers, are taught by the layperson, and they form their own classes and schools. Classrooms now are very different from the past. No longer are there the traditional public school rooms with many desks, but rather they are taught out of people's homes or outdoors in nature, greenhouses or somewhere where students learn useful skills. No longer is the educational system based on competition or grades, but rather on learning and sharing with one another. No more do students fail because they learn slower than other students. And there are no grading systems. As we learn to love more, so do the students.

The public transportation system has improved as well. Transit systems go everywhere and they are more affordable than ever. They have high-speed trains and subways that take minutes to get to the destinations. In fact, some trains that stretch from one side of the world to the other, take a mere few hours to travel back and forth. Traveling by air is almost a thing of the past.

Hospitals have also been converted into education centres for health and nutrition. Not many people nowadays develop diseases as everyone eats wholesome foods full of nutrition.

A lot of people grow the majority of their own food, instead of having lawns or flowers. What is in excess of their own needs, they share or trade with neighbours. What they don't grow, they buy from local farmers' markets. Nothing is mass-produced as no one is eager to waste resources and precious materials. We do with less and buy only when necessary. When we do purchase items, they are either used or fair trade.

As the world starts to heal and the climate begins to stabilize, the weather will eventually be perfect all year round. No more will we experience harsh cold winters or extreme heat and humidity, but warm weather throughout the world, planting fruit trees. Tropical weather will not be a thing we dream about, but it will manifest itself everywhere.

A world like this is very plausible. To us, it seems impossible, only because it is not here, and we always anticipate a dark future. For the majority of us, we can't fathom the world I just painted. We are bombarded with so much violence and suffering, that we believe suffering and death are inevitable and that we are destined to go down a dark path for eons to come. It is because we are in a state of fear that Eden seems inconceivable to most of us. Fear stems from violence, and thus, to eradicate fear, we need to remove the violence from our lives. But not in the traditional way of fighting violence with violence, but instead replacing it with love. We need to create a new system of communities of love and compassion.

The only way to get out of the chaos, is for each one of us to change our beliefs systems, to that of love and compassion for all that lives. I mention this time and time again, because for the truth to sink in, it must be repeated over and over for our psyche to grasp the concept.

In my life, I wonder about the time when we will live in peace and harmony with one another. I know it will happen. I feel that it will manifest in my lifetime. Of course we won't only be interested in spiritual growth, there will also be a time of joy and celebration. Now, because our world is in the transition from darkness to angelic, education and spiritual growth are of utmost importance. But once the majority of humans start awakening, we can devote less time to education and more time for celebrating life with friends and family.

12
Fruitarianism

. . . .

Why Fruit?

Fruit is the flesh around the seed of a fruit-bearing plant. All fruit contain seeds, but not all fruit can be eaten raw. Raw food is never heated. So if you apply heat to food, it is not raw, and therefore, it loses a lot of the life force. Just go ahead and plant any cooked fruit and see if they grow. No cooked food will germinate once heat has been applied to it. Therefore, cooked food is dead food. Yes, that is right, you heard me, it is dead food. Food that is dead cannot grow, because it does not have a life force. All living things have a life-force; moving energy. Though an inanimate object has moving energy, there is no life in the object. It might have had a life before it was a tree (for example).

Everyone wants to live a life where they cause the least harm, and this is where fruits come in. Fruits vibrate at a higher energy frequency compared to all other food. Fruits are the most eco-sustainable and the least harmful. It is hard to find studies and numbers when it comes to comparing different types of foods. Refer to *The Interconnectedness of Life* for more on this.

When we consume the purest diet of fresh, raw, ripe fruit, preferably veganically grown or wild, we work in harmony with nature. If we plant a field of wheat, for example, we usually destroy a forested land, which drives out or kills millions of animals and the biodiversity of life. We till the soil, destroying the earth, killing insects. And then we pour harmful chemicals onto the crops which also destroys the environment while tainting the food supply. Not only that, sometimes the chemicals poison the workers, causing illness. However, when orchards are planted, a home for animal life is created. Otherwise planting almost any other food source will inevitably drive animals away. And if we want animal populations to be in balance with nature, we plant more fruit trees. Fruit trees also help prevent soil erosion and purify the air.[1] When eaten, the seed can be dispersed back into nature to grow another tree. This is a sign of love.

What is so magical about fruits when it comes to diet? Fruits and some vegetables are a high source of vitamin C, while other foods, especially animal and cooked foods are relatively low or absent in vitamin C.[2] Fruits help clean our bodies digestive tract as well as expelling mucus. Externally we can view mucus as earwax and sleep/crust around the eyes and nose. Mucus is caused by eating the wrong food, especially cooked foods.[3] The body cannot utilize anything cooked, or any food other than fruit or vegetable.

Fruit, especially the ones that grow closest to the sun, provide the most energy of any food. When eaten fresh and ripe, fruit leaves us feeling light and energized. For a healthy human, eating solely fruit, it takes at most sixty minutes for the food to digest, while other foods take hours or even days.[4]

Like our planet, a healthy human body is approximately seventy percent water.[5] And thus, we should be eating a diet that contains at least that much water. Fruit (except dried dates and dried fruits) contain at least seventy-four percent water for bananas, ninety-two percent for watermelon and strawberries, ninety-four percent for tomatoes, and ninety-six for cucumbers.[6] Most people around the world, including vegans, are severely dehydrated. Most people eat high fatty cooked meals ladened with oils.

Water - from diet, rather than tap or bottled water - is vital for our bodies. Fruit is number one for that. They help eliminate toxins from our organs, leaving us feeling refreshed, hydrated, and light. Fruit, if eaten on an empty stomach never leaves us feeling heavy or bloated.

Fruitarianism

Fruitarianism is a diet and lifestyle consisting of raw fruit. Fruit are also foods like cucumbers and tomatoes. Some fruitarians also consume vegetables such as leafy greens, which are not technically fruits. Others, such as Mango Wodzak, author of *Destination Eden* and *The Eden Fruitarian Guidebook*, who coined the term 'Eden Fruitarian', eats 100 percent fruit.

> "Eden Fruitarianism is an extension of the philosophy of veganism, embracing the ethics of respect, kindness and compassion for all life on earth, and understanding of mankind's true spiritual nature and physiological needs as a manifested frugivorous species."[7]
>
> **Mango Wodzak,** Author of *Destination Eden* and *The Eden Fruitarian Guidebook*

Can one get all the nutrients from eating fruit only? I have not seen any studies on this yet, but I believe as hominoids, we consumed a diet almost exclusively of fruit. Anthropologists and paleoanthropologists understand that early humans were frugivores.[8] Unlike what our cultural myths tell us, I think humans were in better health back then, compared to today.

Because fruitarianism helps restore the diversity amongst naturally free-roaming animals, it helps restore nature's balance. Forests around the world are destroyed; thus, there is no harmony. Nature has a hard time coping with all the deforestation and destruction we cause with mono-crops of grains and legumes for animal feed and livestock grazing. Even if we were to plant nothing but mono-cultured fruit trees, they would still yield far more food and cause less environmental damage than any other food source.[9]

Just imagine yourself in the heart of the tropics where there are many orchards of different varieties of fruit. You forage through the forest and come upon a mango tree, and you see the delicious edible ripe fruit. The tree produces brightly coloured and sweet smelling fruit so animals will eat them and disperse the seeds upon the ground. In harmony, you pluck the fruit from the branches. There is minimal harm involved in this.

The fruit tree also serves as shade on a hot day. Not many humans and other animals can be all day in direct sun, and thus, shade is essential for keeping cool.

> "What makes fruit so special? That's simple, unlike every other food on this planet, fruit is the only one that has the potential to be grown and harvested with zero harm inflicted."[10]
>
> **Mango Wodzak,** Author of *Destination Eden* and *The Eden Fruitarian Guidebook*

Transitioning to Fruitarianism

Unlike vegetarianism, veganism and fruitarianism are ethical/spiritual lifestyles only attainable through an awakening or several awakenings. A true transformation. The difference between veganism and fruitarianism on ethical-spiritual grounds is that fruitarianism goes further in reducing harm. Although, when one awakens, it is best to transition from the standard diet to veganism first, before proceeding to fruitarianism. The ideal is to go straight to a vegan diet/lifestyle, rather than being vegetarian first. As outlined in this book as well as in *The Interconnectedness of Life*, forgoing only meat (being vegetarian) does not eliminate your participation in the suffering and death of animals caused by humans. It is understandable, that even though most people transition to veganism through vegetarianism, I do not recommend doing so. That is why I highly recommend when making the switch to veganism, include vegan transitional foods, like mock meats, non-dairy milk, honey, and egg substitutes.

When transitioning to fruitarianism, it may take many years or even decades to do so. There is no right or wrong way to do this. In my previous book, I suggest that if one believes they cannot be fully fruitarian, then there is Raw till 4 diet that one can embrace. This is where one consumes all fruit throughout the day with the evening left for a low-fat, high-carb cooked vegan meal.

When I transitioned from the Raw till 4 regimen to full fruitarian, it was hard. After consuming a diet of mostly fruit, one may not even have the inclination to consume greens or nuts and seeds. However, health-wise I understand cooked vegan food leaves me feeling weak. I have less energy and feel bloated whenever I eat heavy meals. Even steamed food leaves me feeling groggy and bloated than if I eat only fruit. I think this is a natural feeling. We are not meant to feel bloated and stuffed. That is why most people cannot eat only fruit because they need to feel that extra fullness in their stomach.

That is why it may take some time before one eliminates the cravings for cooked food altogether. If one still has cravings for cooked vegan foods, enjoy it. Remember though, reduce cooked foods over time, until your body feels no need for them. Eat cooked foods once a day, then eventually once a week, to once a few times a month and then finally to once every few months and so forth, until you don't have a craving for those foods any longer. However, we are all human and if we slip up once in awhile don't fuss over it, but continue doing your best.

Again, eating only fruit is easy. It may take time, but everyone can do it. We thought that veganism was impossible, but now, we see the same hurdles with fruitarianism. It just takes patience and determination, understanding that both veganism and fruitarianism are not merely diets, but ethical-spiritual lifestyles.

I group ethical and spiritual together because once we understand the ethical aspects of the lifestyle we also become more spiritually evolved.

Drugs (Cannabis)

From my research, the cannabis plant has both a few useful benefits as well as some dangerous side effects. The plant has long been used for hemp fibre, hemp seeds, hemp oil for medicinal purposes and as the recreational drug marijuana. From a spiritual perspective, when it comes to marijuana, the experience of being high is not a state that any genuine spiritualist wants to encounter. It distracts the mind and heart from cultivating love and possessing a clear, rational mind. Some people say they do possess a clearer mind, but this is not true.

Any time we use a substance that alters our emotions, thoughts, or actions it indicates that our mind is not pure. If one invites outer influences to affect their psyche, then they cannot remain calm, quiet or have a clear conscience. Any foreign substances that enter the body alters it in a negative way and the consciousness is not pure or free.

When it comes to hemp oils for medicinal purposes, most people take the oil to cure cancers. There is a big difference when it comes to hemp oil sold in stores and the one used as medicine. Even though medicinal hemp oil does cure cancer, people need to realize that there is a core reason these diseases appear in the body in the first place and that it is mostly due to diet related issues.

As mentioned, people succumb to various types of cancers because of eating the wrong foods. Animal foods of any kind lead to a higher risk of certain cancers, including breast, colon, colorectal, prostate, and many others.[11] And so, we need to eliminate the foods that cause the problem in the first place. And then later replace them with foods that fight off cancer cells. Therefore, medicinal hemp oil is a band-aid cure. I go into more detail on the health aspect of a vegan diet in my previous book, *The Interconnectedness of Life*.

Alcohol

I also touch on this subject in my last book, but here I want to address it in further detail. Alcohol causes havoc within the body. It alters brain and heart functionality, even in small doses. No matter the percentage of alcohol in the drink, it is toxic to the human body. It is like pouring less gasoline onto a fire. Even a little is not a good idea if we want to eliminate the fire altogether.

Even if someone feels great after drinking one beer, or glass of wine with their meal, it is not something that any like-minded spiritual person will want to drink. Alcohol produces acid-forming, adverse effects within the body. Because someone feels good after one or two drinks, is not a reason to drink alcohol. People might feel good while on cocaine, but many people understand the harmful effects of the drug. Alcoholic beverages do not benefit the soul, and it is not recommended for spiritual seekers and the awakened ones. At one point in time, our culture and even doctors thought smoking cigarettes was a beneficial thing for the human body. Today many scientific studies confirm that cigarette smoking causes many negative health effects, including lung and throat cancers. There will be a time when scientists say the same thing for alcohol as well.

Many people turn to alcohol for other than social reasons, such as depression, stress, marital issues, and others. As we get older, we are socially accustomed to drinking from our friends and family, and the mainstream media. Alcohol is not something nature provides. It is a human-made concoction, literally poisoning the human body. That is why when we drink too much of it, most people get sick to the point of vomiting. That is a very clear sign that the body rejects the alcohol. The body, as usual, can tolerate a little of it, just like our bodies can tolerate animal foods, however, it is toxic to the body.

As an aware and awakened person transitioning to fruitarianism, you won't need substances or stimulants that alter the body or cause negative reactions within it. Once deciding to take the fruitarian plunge, coffee, cigarettes, marijuana, energy drinks, and pharmaceuticals (unless it is medication for type-1 diabetes), which are clearly not fruit to begin with, are off the list. After awhile, these things will no longer appeal to us.

Again, it may take months, years or decades to transition entirely to fruitarianism. We can't be harsh on ourselves. We must do our best. Undoubtedly, the more fruit we eat, the more incredible we will feel. One tip I highly suggest when transitioning, if you are on the Raw till 4 diet, remember to eat the salad separately from the cooked meal and give it, at least, thirty minutes to digest. Don't forget to eat as much fruit as you wish in the morning and afternoon until you are satiated.

13
Our Journey Continues

. . . .

Veganism is the first step in the journey after a standard animal diet. After that, we transition slowly to fruitarianism. Why should we go fruitarian? Isn't veganism enough? As mentioned in the previous sections, harvesting fruit causes the least harm, especially when comparing it to grains like wheat.

All humans are spiritual, but not everyone is spiritually awake. Some may be partially awake, but people who are not vegan are still unconsciously supporting egregious cruelty and death, and, therefore, cannot be awake. Once people become vegan and experience the awakening, then they may have another awakening or awareness that fruit is the perfect food for human beings. This is where Eden Fruitarianism comes in.

It is an ethical-spiritual lifestyle where one minimizes further harm. And thus, veganism is not yet enough if we want to become esoteric spiritual beings on the earth. A person cannot claim to be spiritually elevated when they still support harm by buying packaged foods like faux cheeses, meats, and other vegan transitional foods. That is what they are for; just to ease the transition for some finding it a challenge to go from being omnivore to vegan. They are not meant to be eaten over a long period of time. They just help people transition to veganism and avoid animal food cravings. However, after years of being vegan, one should look to incorporating more fruit into their diet. Vegan products still cause overall less harm than animal foods, but by no means are they anywhere near the karmicless harm caused by eating fruit alone. If one harvests (ever so gently) fruits from nature, I think there is a possibility to cause no injury at all.

When living a profoundly spiritual life, one has to wonder why long term vegans need to eat foods that look and taste like animals. Packaged foods are extremely toxic to the environment. They are very resource intense, with all the oil and waste they cause. They are not health food, as they usually contain more than a dozen ingredients. From a health perspective, when one chooses to consume foods that contain more than two ingredients, it causes havoc within the body. Our bodies are delicate, and, therefore, are meant to eat one food at a time, or at most three or four when making a salad for example. Especially when it comes to oils and foods that cause bad breath, like garlic and onion.

Oils are highly processed 100 percent fat.[1] They are also empty calories; meaning they have little to no nutritional value.[2] Most oils contain too many omega-6.[1] We should be getting more omega-3 than 6, and so the answer is not to consume oils and add in flax or chia seeds to our diets, but eliminate omega-6 all together and forget taking band-aid cures.

The reason garlic and onions cause bad breath is because it is a sign that these foods should not be eaten in the first place. No food should leave an after smell in the gut and breath. Which causes one to have foul breath. If a person's excrement has a strong odour, it is a sign that they are not eating the right types of food.

Eating a diet predominately of fruit and vegetables (I believe even fruit alone) can supply the body with an adequate amount of omega-3. Of course, children need more fat than adults, and thus, avocados and durians are good foods to add to their diets. Decrease the fat content gradually until they reach their early to mid-teens. I am not a rigorous person who adheres to the 80/10/10 diet (eighty percent minimum calories from carbohydrates, and maximum ten percent calories from fats and protein). In certain cases, people may need a little more fat, if they live in a colder climate, especially during the winter months. Therefore, I recommend up to fifteen percent fat in one's diet. I understand fat above this level to be detrimental to one's health. The average vegan who eats foods high in oils, and a lot of cooked foods, averages forty-two percent of calories from fat. Omnivores eat this much fat as well.[3] And no matter where the fat comes from, too much fat is too much.[4] Most raw vegans average sixty to eighty percent fat, using a lot of oils and nuts in their recipes; consuming most of their fats as omega-6.[5]

That is why a lot of vegans are still having health issues. I highly recommend removing all oils from one's diet and instead include some avocados. For people trying to lose weight, they need to limit their fat to five to ten percent, until the weight falls off. Eating a diet of fruit and vegetables only, contains all the fat, and protein our bodies ever need. When we consume grape seed oil for example, where do we get the oil from? The oil is extracted from the grapes, thus, oil is heavily refined and processed human-made concoction, no matter what it says on the bottle. And thus, we should be eating the grapes alone and getting all the nutrients from them. Just like we should be eating the grapes and forgo the wine.

Once people understand the detrimental health effects of oils and cooked foods, they can start adding more fruit to their diet. Again fruitarianism is an ethical-spiritual lifestyle and not merely a diet. Love is the heart of it. Once we love all life, including our own, we won't want to put anything into our body that is not pure. Because we will be harming ourselves if we do. Fruit is the only pure food there is.

Again, when I talk about fruitarianism, I am always referring to Eden Fruitarians: those who get 100 percent - or close to - of their calorie from fruit. So, when we are on this path, we are on the right side. This lifestyle is one of the easiest if you are living in a supportive environment and are surrounded by like-minded people.

I would highly suggest moving to the tropics and finding other fruitarians or, at least, ones who eat predominately fruit and are ethically/spiritually like-minded. This will be the best way to stay fruitarian and not resort to some cooked food.

I understand that cooked food is addicting, and so if one continues to consume cooked food even on occasion, then most likely they go back to eating almost entirely cooked, especially if they were not ethically and spiritually motivated in the first place. One has to resist peer pressure from friends and family and adhere to their morals. This is hard in a society that pressures us into eating the wrong foods.

Here are a few tips and ideas for staying fruitarian.

1. Take enough fruit, whenever you are out, so you don't end up hungry or eating junk food. Pack fruit that doesn't spoil, such as, pears, apples, oranges, tangerines or any harder type fruit. Always carry a large backpack just in case you go grocery shopping. This way you won't be tempted to eat unhealthy food.

2. Keep a large quantity of ripe and unripe fruit around your home so you won't be tempted to eat other foods.

3. Do not be lazy. Take time to shop and find high quality tasty fruit.

4. Buy fruit in season, for best taste and better prices.

5. Purchase both ripe and unripe fruit, so all the fruit doesn't ripen at the same time, risking spoilage.

6. Buy the highest quality fruit you can find within your budget. An experienced fruitarian can usually tell if a fruit will become ripe or if a fruit is better tasting or not. Remember not everyone has access to the best fruits around, so do your best when grocery shopping.

7. If you have the means, start your own veganic fruit orchard or pick wild fruit.

8. Do not fuss, if you cannot find organic or veganic produce. Again, do the best you can. Even if you can only buy or afford conventional produce, that is great. Conventional fruit is far healthier than any other food.

9. Do not store anything but fruit in your home. Because when one has other kinds of foods around the house, there is a temptation to eat those foods, especially if they are high in fat and salt.

10. When going to someone's place, remember to tell them ahead of time that you only eat fruit. Most people will have fruit at their place, but maybe not ripe fruit and so it is best to eat ahead of time, and also bring your food just in case. I never leave my home without my backpack and some fruit to last

me a few hours.

11. It is hard to go out to restaurants when you only eat fruit. But most restaurants will be happy to make a fruit smoothie. Call the restaurant in advance to be sure.

12. If you are out, and there is no fruit around, don't make that an excuse to eat animal foods. There are many places where vegans can eat. Search for a local vegan restaurant on the internet or go to your nearest supermarket or health store.

14
The World is Crying

. . . .

Nonhuman animals get sad, just as humans do. Humans generally don't appreciate this fact. There is a lack of caring for, and acknowledgement of, the feelings of animals. And that is where the problem lies, our ego. It is being indifferent to other beings. That is why we are violent to each other and cause destruction to the earth.

Will we ever learn from our mistakes? Not if we continue to eat butchered animals and their secretions. The most alarming statistic that I heard many years ago, is that by 2048 all life in the oceans will be gone.[1] But what does this mean? It means a demise for our species. And if people still do not care, it is likely because ego is taking over and ego does not foresee a bright future. It sees a dark future for all life.

This is the way we are programmed since birth. And still for some vegans they retain some of the old programming habits. And even if we are awakened to the morality of veganism, we may still have tendencies which are not vegan. And so we must with all our heart dismantle old thought and habit patterns of our earlier omnivore days. It is tough, especially the older we get the more conditioned we are.

As I think back to the photo of me beside the bear at the circus, I still cannot believe why I had a hard time understanding that I was the problem. I knew there was an issue, but I thought it was out there in the world, and that it had nothing to do with me. Again, we blame others. We blame Governments and corporations and ask them to solve the problems. But how can they when it is only love that heals everything? Nothing can get us out of the mess, but love.

The earth is also dying. She calls out to us, begging for mercy. In return, she lashes out with tornadoes, floods, droughts, and other catastrophes. We see the aftermath of all the destruction we are causing, yet we sit silently doing nothing about it. We say yes to technology that might save us, yet the only thing that can, is love. We always want a pill or technology for a quick fix. In fact, we should be saving ourselves. We got in this mess; now we have to fix it.

We have become a virus plundering the earth for all the resources. We think resources last forever and wonder why countries are going bankrupt, and prices are ever skyrocketing. We keep killing, yet we keep calling for peace. We need to realize the time for peace is now. Peace is the long ignored but obvious solution.

All this suffering, and we consider ourselves intelligent and wise? Aren't wise people supposed to have empathy for others and treat other beings with love and compassion? How about all the forest fires and droughts? Where will we turn to next? What will we destroy, and who will we destroy? If anything is in our path, and we don't like it, we annihilate it.

What do we think about the idea of the destruction of factory farms and laboratories? Even though the Animal Liberation Front (ALF) has never harmed a single living being, in my view causing property damage is not the way to go about getting the message out to the public. Violence, even to property, just leads to more violence. Though the actions reach the media outlets, and activists save a few animals, it conveys a negative message about veganism. Yes, I am very grateful when a few animals are protected, but in the end, if there is still demand for animal products, they will be available.

Violence begets violence, even if it is directed at property. Negative and hateful thoughts and emotions are sent out to the universe, and it boomerangs back to us as violence. We are not here to fight, we are here to love and to build a new world, based on sharing, compassion, and love for all.

15
Is Hunting the Solution?

. . . .

I agree that hunting may have been acceptable, tens of thousands of years ago for our survival, but today in our modern world we don't need animal products for sustenance. There are plenty of plant-based foods available. Every animal we kill, we end their life. And they don't want to die prematurely, just like we wouldn't want to be killed. We are destroying the fabric of life. Every time we kill, we harm ourselves; we consume their blood, their muscles, their tendons, and their spirit. And then on top of that we disguise the food, by removing their eyes, face, tail, skin and then we cook their body, maybe bread it, spice it, add vegetables, and sauces and condiments. We disguise it because we cannot bear to look at the dead corpse of an animal.

If we were true carnivores, or even omnivores, we would be consuming their flesh raw like other animals do. But we don't. We cook and tenderize their bodies. Animals eat other animals in nature, so why can't we? Thus, we mimic carnivorous animals in nature, and we pick and chose what we want to copy from their lifestyle. Lions do not consume chicken eggs, milk or cheese. Also, many carnivorous animals greet one another by sniffing each other's butts. People don't tend to practice such behaviours. Just like from the Bible, we pick and chose what we want to believe to be true, such as 'Thou shall not kill'.

Without tools, we cannot rip and chew through the hide of the animal. Even road kill is repulsive to us, with all the flies around the dead carcass and the putrid smell. Most people don't want anything to do with it. Maybe what prevents people from thinking about where the flesh, dairy, and eggs in the stores come from, is because they are packaged nicely. They look clean and sanitized and far removed from the reality of where they are from. Consumers don't know what goes on behind the closed doors of the farms and slaughterhouses. [read *The Interconnectedness of Life* to learn more about this].

Children and families watch videos of farmers picking apples. Heck, they even go to the orchards and see how it's done, and they even pick their own. Do you think anyone would want a visit to a slaughterhouse to kill an animal for their dinner, or even let their children be witness to such violence?

When we see an injured dog or baby bird on the street, we try to assist them. Do we ever salivate and want to munch on their bodies? No. Why? Because it is repulsive. We don't have that inclination. Only true carnivores have this instinct. Our western culture teaches us to eat certain animals and their secretions. Why don't we drink milk from buffalos or camels or eat eggs from different bird species, other than chicken? Why don't we consume dog and cat meat? Why are we so picky with what we eat? If humans were true carnivores, we wouldn't care which animal or animal products we eat. And they call vegans picky.

If we were biological carnivores and hunters, we would be salivating and killing our pray without modern equipment and only with our bare hands, running and catching the animal and eating them raw, right in nature with everything intact: their tails, eyes, skin, nose, everything. I guarantee, virtually no one would have the inclination to do so. Aborigines hunt animals, and it takes hours and sometimes even days to track down the animal to kill him/her. They run after them until the animal is exhausted, no longer able to run.[1] I don't think in this modern day and age; anyone would want to pursue that.

What it comes down to is the idea of using and killing another being that is the problem. Not how we treat them. We all know that deep down, that killing is evil.

We are in the mess because of violence. It doesn't matter who the victim is or how gently we kill them. There is a morality that is innate in human consciousness. No one has to tell us, not to steal money from the old man. No one has to explain to us, not to rob a store, or not to kick the puppy or not to rape another. Because the majority of us are decent human beings, who understand the difference between right and wrong.

The only reason anyone is eating animal foods is because we were forced by our culture to do so as infants. Our parents and all institutions taught us that it is okay to do so and that certain animals are here for our use, and some are for our love.

I have repeated myself many times, as people are still delusional. The planet is being utterly devastated, and nonhuman animals are used, tortured, and slaughtered. Even backyard raised animals and hunting are not viable and sustainable options.[2] We will never be able to feed a hungry world with the number of animals killed.

We cannot create a peaceful and loving world if we are still violent. There is no way around that. Wake up. This world is not going to get any better, as long as we see other animals as property. Animals are not property or disposable units. They are not here to feed us or to be used in any way. They are sentient beings that have the innate right to live free lives in their natural environments. We have no reason to be breeding animals, and doing as we please with them.

There will still be people who will justify using and hunting animals. There is still no excuse for murdering another living being. If I were in a dire situation, living somewhere high in the mountains or the forest all alone, I would still protect the ecology and not harm animals. Of course, there are very rare situations where people need to kill animals to survive. Even in those circumstances, I think it is very immoral.

We are not living a subsistence lifestyle any longer and even if we were, humans are ideally tropical beings. If we have the means, we should move somewhere warmer and more abundant with fruit.

If one is still adamant about viewing animals as property and killing them for food or using them for other purposes, then they haven't awakened to love. Thank you to any of those people who are open-minded enough to have read this far into the book. Planting seeds of love and compassion is all we can do. That is our job; to raise global consciousness of humanity.

"The stage that humankind has now reached would allow us to live much more healthfully if we moved away from animal consumption and animal by-products such as dairy, eggs and honey. Then the mass murder in our physical culture will decrease, our illnesses will vastly reduce, and we will literally create world peace in our hearts."[3]
Kim Deborah Benson (Presh)

16

The Vision for the Future

· ·

It is somewhere in the far distant future. People are now living in small communities out in nature. We share and work with each other and do not own anything. We gather food from the orchards or grow whatever we cannot find. As humans, we decided it was time to let go of our old ways of existing in exchange for a new way where we live in harmony with all life. We never kill another being, as we get all our nourishment from plants alone.

Our entire herding culture is disbanded, for a new way of life. Shopping malls, governments, corporations and our old ways, are a thing of the past. No longer do we have the need for any possessions, as we share with one another. All that is needed is food to sustain ourselves. No longer is there a need for vehicles, telephones or technology. Most of us moved back to the tropics where we live in close-knit communities with our friends and family.

Schools and modern educational systems are things of the past, as we all learn from one another. Hospitals and all institutions are non-existent in our world. No one ever takes anything from the land, unless they give back. We listened to our hearts, finally going back to our traditional ways of living in nature.

No longer is there inequality or slavery. There is peace, love, and harmony amongst us all. Who decides on rules and how people should live? No one does. It is our hearts of pure love, that dictates this. There are some who just go through life frolicking in the meadows and orchards all day; while others continue to be creative with their hobbies and talents. It is not as if we totally abandoned our purposes just for nature. Some of us still paint, build things, write, or put on shows and entertainment. But instead of letting ego and materialism get in the way of it, we let love grab hold. Love, compassion, and Mother Earth are our guidance and teachers.

We are now living in Eden. It is a beautiful garden full of love and compassion. No monocultures of grains, no dead animals, no suffering or violence of any sort. There are no illnesses and diseases, because people consume a pure fruit diet. Alcohol, recreational and pharmaceutical drugs, tobacco, stimulants and all frivolous and impractical ideals, are long gone from our memories. No longer do we plunder the earth, but rather appreciate our home. We take care of her. We sit with other animals, in harmony. They come to us, not afraid, and we both enjoy each other's company. Though we believe that this lifestyle is humdrum, full of boredom, as we get back to living in harmony with all life, we will experience much joy and happiness.

There is no need for any material possessions, jobs, fame, money, or prestige. As love and happiness are all we ever need. Even as vegans, we were harming the earth with all the plastics and garbage and with non-sustainable farming practices. As our hearts awakened to love, something magically happened. We all united and left home. Leaving home, was the pinnacle of it, as we no longer wanted to live a life of harm.

For me, it is easy to live on fruit. As I gently plucked the edible food from the tree, I immersed myself in the interconnectedness of all life. I have arrived at the conclusion that this is the reason I exist. There is oneness in all that exists. All understanding and truth come from within, and as time lingers on, and we sense a deep appreciation and compassion from within, we also feel love.

We have lost this love, and that is why *The Lost Love* is to reawaken the innate love and compassion that has been hidden and suppressed within ourselves for decades. It is now time that we reawaken the love and cultivate it into our lives. Not only in theory but in practice as well. We need love to flourish; otherwise we will not experience a loving and peaceful world. And that is what we all long for.

It is not enough that we find *The Lost Love*, we have to nurture it at the deepest level of our being. Love is the solution, the answer to everything. And because it has been absent from our lives for so many years, it is now time that we embrace it wholeheartedly. We need to include every living thing in our circle of compassion and embrace them with love. This is the only way to ensure our survival. There is no way to peace, but to be at peace ourselves. If we want a loving world, we need to create that within. Our whole being must be pure unconditional love, which is the highest form of love/energy.

As we see our world as Eden, there is no violence, no competition, and no negativity. These things only lead us away from Eden. If we want there to be an Eden, we must bring Eden back. And if we are ever going to understand the real meaning of existence, and why we even came to be, we need to rise consciously to a new spiritual level, that of unimaginable proportions. This life is waiting for us. Eden is needed in our time of crises. Our world is shattered; it is falling apart, and we are all dying of terrible loneliness and diseases. Today is the day that we shall begin to reawaken *The Lost Love* within ourselves, and embrace it wholeheartedly with all living creatures.

Afterword

· · · · · · · · · · · ·

It is very easy to eat cruelty-free. Preparing delicious food of love, directly grown from nature is a blessing. In today's world anyone can eat plants and find enough plant-foods to sustain themselves. The animals don't need our excuses, whining or crying. They just need us to stop eating and using them. That is all that they want. And when that happens, then will they want to sit down and cuddle next to us. No one wants to cuddle next to a mass murderer. And that is what we are: killers and rapists, the worst virus on the planet.

But there is great news. People can change. We don't have to continue being cruel and violent to others. All we need to do is embrace that one little thing in our lives called love. Love will solve everything. No, I am not drifting on a cloud or dreaming of la-la land. In fact, I am very aware of what is happening on the planet today. If someone is still part of the herding culture, they are the ones who are unaware.

People call me naïve, extreme, and fanatical. It is because they can't face the cold hard truth. Their ego gets in the way. They cannot admit that they are the ones who are causing pain and suffering in this world. Instead, they criticize, judge, and shame me. Criticizing me for loving animals and the earth?

Any time anyone's beliefs are scrutinized; they always end up being defensive. And that is what they are, only beliefs. Just like religion is only a belief. They are not the truth because truth has to come from the heart, not from external forces.

We have to embrace a kinder life. It is the only sensible thing to do. What do we see when we enter a supermarket? Almost always, we are greeted with the glorious fresh, sweet, aroma, and beauty of fruit and vegetables. Then as we walk further into the store, past the produce section, we get to the packaged and processed foods, and then we are greeted with the sight of dismembered body parts and secretions of animals. You see the difference in colour? Plants contain a wide range of bright colours, while animal flesh is red like a bloody cemetery.

Many years ago, when I first started writing, I knew that writing would be my purpose in life. I am so fortunate to be given this life where I can utilize my talents for helping others. Like me, millions of vegans and fruitarians around the world are contributing to a kinder and more compassionate world for everyone.

For me, it started in 2009 when I became vegan, and ever since that time I kept adding more fruit to my diet. Today, my diet is virtually all fruit-based. I love animals and the Earth dearly, and thus do not want to cause any harm.

I love fruit. I love music, especially ambient and electronic, and often listen while meditating and writing. One thing that has helped me on my path to fruitarianism is Mango Wodzak's books.

Until we fully accept fruit as our only real food source, we will never be alive to experience and appreciate this world. Until we migrate to the tropics and have access to fruit all year round, we will still be in a battle with our conscience. Growing veganic fruit or cultivating wild fruit are simply better in quality and taste. Thus, when we consume nothing but the highest quality plant foods, fresh, ripe, and raw, we bring our energy levels and spirits to a new dimension.

Of course, with technology, we can grow food all year round in colder climates, but it is not ideal to be taking vitamin D supplements and eating store-bought produce. I admit, though, store-bought produce is still better than other foods, if that is all one can afford to purchase. However, most people reading this book and using the internet, are clearly in a position to move to the tropics. Not only are the tropics where we are designed to live, but it is also home to some of the most delicious exotic fruit around.

As we read, animal products cause tremendous suffering, so fill your face with all the plants you wish. You have no time to lose. According to various numbers floating around, vegans save fifty to a hundred animals per year, just by being vegan. And that number does not include aquatic animals or insects, and thus, vegans save hundreds or even thousands of animals annually.[1]

We can save even more animals once we start educating people around us. There is no time to lose.

What is needed is as many people to help spread the compassionate and loving lifestyle to others. This is how positive change is created.

The world is in a dire situation, and right now we are at the tipping point. The situation is, even more, urgent and fatal than we ever imagined it. We need everyone's assistance to spread this valuable information to the world. When you finish reading, tell everyone about the urgency. It doesn't matter what they say, or how ignorant they are. Give this book to others and buy multiple copies for your friends and family for the festive seasons and birthdays.

Sometimes one may get frustrated that the majority of people don't listen, or they never change. As Howard Lyman - a fourth generation cattle rancher, and author of *Mad Cowboy* - expressed it at the 2007 Animal Rights Conference in Washington, DC:

"If you don't think we can make changes, ask yourself, how about that damn crazy ex-cattleman? I mean if that guy can change, anybody can change. We can make a difference and remember, eighty percent of Americans are brain dead. They're part of the heard; they are following nose to tail, and when you follow nose to tail there is only one thing you see in front of you [the ass of the guy in front of you]. Forget about trying to reform Joe six-pack. I mean there are certain things you just cannot do. But don't worry about the eighty percent that are brain dead, because when the majority of the twenty percent that are thinking where they're going to go, the eighty percent soon will follow."[2]

I want to thank everyone for reading this book. Visit the following website for additional books, information, and to follow me.

www.weareinterconnected.com

References

· · · · · · · · · · · · ·

Chapter 1: Interconnectedness

1. Braden, Gregg. *The Divine Matrix*. http://amzn.to/1XMGbfI
2. Braden Gregg, *The Divine Matrix*. Video conference, Milano Italy. May 30, 2007.
3. Conservation of Energy. Wikipedia.org http://bit.ly/1rhjphn
4. Benson, Kim Deborah (Presh). The Perfect Food, Vegan Coach. https://youtu.be/qwFP07A2DWs
5. Bite Size Vegan. What's our Number? https://youtu.be/fcBJLpF1xFs
6. Andre, Claire and Velasquez. World Hunger: A Moral Response. http://bit.ly/24GR7ty
7. The Facts, Cowspiracy: The Sustainable Secret (Documentary). www.cowspiracy.com/facts
8. Monson, Shaun, Unity (Audiobook). http://bit.ly/unityaudiobook
9. Eisnitz, Gail, *Slaughterhouse* (2006) (ePUB version). pp. 131, 132. http://amzn.to/1PoLc5B
10. Shell Ethics, Studies Link Slaughterhouses to Violent Crimes Increase. http://bit.ly/1UNOZL8
11. Tolstoy, Leo. A Calendar of Wisdom, July 20. http://amzn.to/1tnJBsv

Chapter 2: Do Plants Feel Pain?

1. Yacoubou, Jeanne, MS, Factors Involved in Calculating Grain: Meat Conversion Ratios. http://bit.ly/25XvGHh
2. Benson, Kim Deborah (Presh). The Perfect Food, Vegan Coach. https://youtu.be/qwFP07A2DWs
3. Shelomi, Matan, PhD, Why Don't Plants Have Brains or

Nervous System? Quora. http://bit.ly/234SMtO
4. Tuttle, Will, PhD, A Case for The World Peace Diet, Supreme Master Television. https://youtu.be/gzu9P-nwN10

Chapter 3: Owning Animals
1. History of Animal Testing. Wikipedia.org
    http://bit.ly/25SWLLQ
2. Brown, Harold. Peaceable Kingdom: The Journey Home (2009). http://peaceablekingdomfilm.org

Chapter 5: Can We Cope in This Crazy World?
1. Ravikant, Kamal, *Love Yourself Like Your Life Depends On It.* http://amzn.to/1rhuaQz

Chapter 6: Unconscious Spirituality
1. Schwartz, Richard H., The Case Against Eating Fish, NAVS (North American Vegetarian Society). http://bit.ly/1VV5jPi

Chapter 7: Natural Laws
1. Natural Law, Wikipedia.org
    https://en.wikipedia.org/wiki/Natural_law
2. The Principles of Natural Law
    https://www.youtube.com/playlist?list=PLrIvkvk1x8zOJEct
    HpDn9xcJNRK-Hjb6I

Chapter 8: The Meaning of Life
1. Monson, Shaun, Unity (The audiobook).
    http://bit.ly/unityaudiobook

Chapter 10: Awakening
1. The Vegan Society, Vegan Society Articles of Association (2016). http://bit.ly/veganarticleassociation, p. 2

Chapter 12: Fruitarianism
1. Hansen, Jolene, Tropical Fruit Trees to Prevent Soil Erosion.

SFGATE. http://bit.ly/28xnobq

2. Thomas MD, Liji, Sources of Vitamin C. As seen on News Medical website from the chart, animal foods are relatively low in vitamin C, especially when cooked, and most animal foods contain no vitamin C. Best sources of vitamin C come from fruits and vegetables. http://bit.ly/1sCgDoe

3. Wodzak, Mango, *The Eden Fruitarian Guidebook*, Section Two: Transitioning, Victimisation, The Common Cold. p. 196.

4. Optimal Food Combining, Optimum Health Institute. http://bit.ly/1UqyTey

5. Follow the Water: Finding the Perfect Match for Life, NASA Fact Sheet, NASA. http://go.nasa.gov/1tmy2B8

6. Water Amounts in Fruits and Vegetables, RRTCDD (The Rehabilitation Research and Training Center on Development Disabilities and Health) http://bit.ly/21h5ofV

7. Wodzak, Mango. http://fruitnut.net

8. Science Verifies That Humans' Ancestors Were Frugivores, Scribd. http://bit.ly/humansarefrugivores

9. Wodzak, Mango, *Destination Eden.* Environmental Issues, Agriculture p. 107. Section Four: Additional Related Thoughts, Food Supply, Fruit Trees p. 202

10. Wodzak, Mango, *The Eden Fruitarian Guidebook*. Section One: Defining Eden Fruitarian, The Uniqueness of Fruit. p. 32.

11. Physicians Committee for Responsible Medicine, Meat Consumption and Cancer Risk. http://bit.ly/pcrmcancer

Chapter 13: Our Journey Continues

1. Cronometer. https://cronometer.com

2. Knutson, Patty, Vegan Coach
www.vegancoach.com/nutrition-for-a-vegan.html

3. Graham, Douglas, Dr., *The 80/10/10 Diet* (2010 PDF Version). How Much Fat Do We Eat? pp. 77, 78

4. Food Choices Documentary. www.foodchoicesmovie.com

5. Graham, Douglas, Dr., *The 80/10/10 Diet* (2010 PDF Version). Chapter 8 – The Big Surprise: Raw Fooders Average 60%+ Fat! pp. 80, 81

Chapter 14: The World is Crying

1. Seafood May Be Gone by 2048, Study Says, National Geographic. http://bit.ly/1U3jH3k

Chapter 15: Is Hunting the Solution

1. BBC, Life of Mammals. https://youtu.be/826HMLoiE_o
2. Lanfield, Michael, What About Backyard Animal Farming? Is it Ethical? Moral? https://youtu.be/M4ySbSC12uo
3. Benson, Kim Deborah (Presh). The Perfect Food, Vegan Coach. https://youtu.be/qwFP07A2DWs

Afterword

1. Counting Animals, How Many Animals Does a Vegetarian Save? http://bit.ly/countinganimals
2. Lyman, Howard. Animal Right Conference 2007. https://youtu.be/Z_dWPwjs6dA

Made in the USA
Columbia, SC
09 October 2017